AIRE ~~ ~~ **SUEZ**

Sandy Cavenagh
Jan 2006.

AIRBORNE TO SUEZ

Sandy Cavenagh

Foreword by
Field Marshal the Viscount Montgomery of Alamein
K.G., G.C.B., D.S.O.

GLUDY PUBLICATIONS

First published in 1965 by
William Kimber and Co, Limited

Re-published in 1996 with additional photographs by
Gludy Publications, Brecon, Powys

ISBN 0 9528786 0 7

The proceeds from the publication of this edition will
be donated to the Airborne Forces Security Fund

Produced by
The Choir Press, Gloucester GL1 1SP
Printed in Great Britain

CONTENTS

To the memory of Corporal Wood, Private Barnett, Private Bates and Private Summers, who were killed at Port Said; and to all who established and who maintain the tradition of Airborne Forces.

FOREWORD

by Field Marshall the Viscount Montgomery of Alamein,
K.G., G.C.B., D.S.O.

I have read this book with the greatest interest, and not only because the author is known to me and was at Winchester with my son. It begins with the story of the operations of a Parachute Battalion against Grivas and the murder gangs in Cyprus, that unhappy island which was for so long in the grip of political unrest. This story bears a marked similarity to the operations of British soldiers in the struggle with the Sinn Fein in Ireland in 1921, which developed into a murder campaign in which we British so dislike being involved.

The battalion, in which the author was the Medical Officer, was then suddenly uprooted and parachuted into Egypt as the spearhead of the British contribution in the Suez operation of November 1956. The few comments which the author makes about the bewildering political scene of those days are more than justified, as I know well; so also are his remarks about the chaotic state of affairs on mobilisation, and the lack of trained men and proper equipment. The true story of the Suez muddle has yet to be told; and when that day comes the story will not reflect with credit on the British Government of those days nor on the Chiefs of Staff.

But what will interest the reader so much, as it did me, is that, throughout, the story is told from the point of view of the regimental officers and men of his battalion—those who in the end win the battle, however good may be the higher leading, or however bad. The author, who himself took part

7

in the events described, has pieced them together into a tale of human endeavour and suffering by young soldiers which is up to the highest standards of the British Army. He brings out clearly the relationship between man and man, a human relationship on which is founded the success of a battalion (and of an army) in times of stress; indeed, therein lies the foundation of leadership—the relationship between man and man.

For these reasons alone the book should have a good sale. Indeed, I hope this may happen because all the royalties are to be given to the charities of the Airborne Forces.

Montgomery of Alamein
F. M.

ISLINGTON MILL,
ALTON.
April 1965.

AUTHOR'S PREFACE

So many people have helped to write this story that it is impossible to acknowledge them all individually. But I hope that each member of the 16th Independent Parachute Brigade may be able to recognise his contribution in the narrative. At the same time I know how many other people and incidents should have been included in the book. To those involved, who also know, I can only apologise for the innumerable omissions.

A Parachute Battalion is a bewilderingly large family. Therefore to simplify the task of remembering names and positions, an appendix is included which should enable the reader to pinpoint most of the the characters who appear in the story.

I should like particularly to thank Major General M. A. H. Butler, C.B., C.B.E., D.S.O., M.C., and Brigadier P. E. Crook, D.S.O., O.B.E., for their advice on the narrative, and Colonel J. P. F. Miles, D.S.O., and Mr. H. Gresswell for their constructive criticisms of the typescript. Equally my thanks are due to my brother R. Q. Cavenagh for preparing the maps, and to Miss C. J. Rowlands for typing and re-typing the manuscript.

PREFACE TO SECOND EDITION

FORTY years on, Suez is no longer an issue to bring down a Prime Minister. Yet the retreat from Empire it was widely held to signify, and the subsequent relinquishing of many of our international responsibilities has not brought about a corresponding reduction in our military obligations. Since the first edition of this book was published 9 years after the events of 1956, British Airborne Forces, and the Parachute Regiment in particular, have been almost continuously involved in peace-keeping operations on the home front in Northern Ireland, in several UN missions overseas, and one remarkable feat of arms in the Falklands. The cost has been high. Since 1956 the Parachute Regiment has had 217 men killed and about 10 times that number injured and wounded. It has also survived intermittent threats of reduction and even disbandment. What has become clear, however, is that the regimental traditions that were so much in evidence 40 years ago are every bit as vital to the nation's interest now as they were then. These have undoubtedly been further ingrained by more exhaustive selection procedures, intensive training in a wider variety of roles and the mastery of new weaponry and other equipment. The claim that the Falklands was won 'on the training area of Sennybridge' is substantially correct (although the Argentinians had better night sights than 2 and 3 Para), as the leadership qualities of NCOs have improved immeasurably as a result of the School of Infantry's efforts in Wales in training sergeants and corporals to take command when officers become casualties—perhaps a greater hazard in the Paras then elsewhere in the Army.

The regiment's activities read like a brochure of an—almost certainly unsuccessful—travel agent. Since 1965 there have been operations in Guyana, Brunei and Malaysia, Zanzibar, Cyprus, South Arabia, Aden, Das island, Northern Ireland (27 tours in all), Anguila, Dhofar, Hong Kong, Zimbabwe, the New Hebrides, Sinai, Belize, the Falkland Islands, Lebanon, Uganda and Iraq. Most of these operations have been of short duration, many of them unpredictable, and it is worth pausing to think what it is like to be the wife or family of a soldier whose life is liable to such disruption.

Inevitably there have been mistakes and successes, triumphs and tragedies—and accidents galore. It is simply no use expecting parachute soldiers to pussy-foot around when action of any sort is called for—the only sensible conclusion to be drawn from the ill-conceived 'war crimes' investigation in the Falklands. 'The Commandos think about it and then go and get killed, the Paras just go and get killed' was somebody's comment on that campaign. The mounting list of awards for bravery tells the same story; several of them—invariably the highest—are posthumous. I shall never forget attending in 1990, the 50th anniversary dinner to celebrate the formation of Airborne Forces in London's Guildhall, and there, among the 600 officers present, I reflected that seldom, if ever, can so many decorations for gallantry have been worn under one roof. More sobering to think that they represented the surviving tip of an iceberg

Alastair Pearson, the legendary much decorated and outspoken battalion commander in World War II put forward one of his soldiers twice for the award of V.C. 'Twice mark you! and he ended up with f... all'.

The Toms humour has carried this a stage further 'what happens to Paras when they go to hell?'

'They just regroup and break out'

As a GP in Brecon I have been lucky in following the fortunes of 'the Paras' at close quarters, and today the bonds of forty years ago are as close as ever. Many of the officers of

3 Para have gone on to high command in the army, a number are captains of industry or leading members of their subsequent professions, but our reunions wipe away all this and we are back in Tunisia Camp near Nicosia as if it were yesterday. Erosion of the ranks of those who landed on El Gamil airfield is now due to advancing years and disease rather than trauma, but 200-plus have been meeting at five-yearly intervals to dine and renew old friendships in Aldershot, and it is out of this group that the idea of setting the record straight was born. Thanks to this initiative and the greater objectivity that a long-term historical perspective inevitably permits, what Monty referred to in his foreword as 'the true story of the Suez muddle' is about to unfold.

Three BM Television, an independent production company is about to produce for the BBC a documentary, 'The Suez Crisis', in which many surviving participants have been interviewed. The production team have ranged world-wide in their search for personalities from political, military and media spheres and they have visited most of the sites involved. Some of those who took part in the battle will be interviewed against the background of their deeds. Such is the power of television that this should be the final re-write of what is now viewed as the nadir of British foreign policy. 'History is a capricious creature. It depends on who writes it', was Gorbachev's conclusion recently. We must be grateful that the full story, objectively researched, is about to be published.

Paul Crook, our distinguished Commanding Officer in 1956, together with a number of officers, NCO's and men, in which I was privileged to be included, were brought together by Mike Walsh in January 1996 for a series of interviews held in Aldershot with the production team under the direction of Jeremy Bennett. In the 2 Para Officers' Mess we were quizzed microscopically on our experiences in 1956, and it dredged a lot of hidden memories to the surface. Being surrounded at lunch by the lean, fit, keen young men who

12

run 2 Para today was a poignant reminder of the passing of time. Only Pompey Norman, who swims across Portsmouth harbour daily, has remained in their league.

I was doubly fortunate, for taken in company with Don Hayward, sometime Corporal in B company, we returned to Port Said in March to re-visit the scene. We flew to Cairo and then travelled by minibus to Ismailia in the hopes that filming of the Canal and Port Said by helicopter would be possible. True to form the weather decreed otherwise, with a high wind and a dust storm. This plan had to be abandoned until later. When we finally reached El Gamil we found the only surviving building from 1956 to be the old airport control tower, due for demolition in 3 months time. It was eerie to retrace Francois' footsteps up the rusting staircase, being followed in turn by the film cameraman to the roof and view the scene. The runway is much lengthened and new airport reception buildings are mushrooming. Busy helicopter traffic flies to off-shore oil rigs, and old radar installations cover much of the south border of the airfield. The sewage farm is considerably reduced by the lengthened runway, and the road into Port Said is now a busy dual carriageway. The cemetery and flats are more or less unchanged, but much of Lake Manzala has been reclaimed and built over.

But the most touching part of the visit occurred the next day when two of our old adversaries, Mr Salem Sakr and Mr Zachariah, joined us for interview. Salem Sakr commanded the company defending the east end of the airfield and Zachariah was wounded by Sergeant Vokes's patrol. He had full RAMC documentation to detail his treatment in the airfield garage by Maurice Fearnley and the Field Ambulance, by Norman Kirby's surgical team, and later on HMS Eagle and in Limassol, Cyprus. A feat of record-keeping to which the NHS might well aspire. Salem Sakr's English is very good. Some parts of the interview were light-hearted and dissolved in laughter, but the serious undercurrent reflecting the mood of 1956 came to the fore when he described the lethal hide-and-seek in the cemetery —from the Egyptain point of view.

The Union Jack and the French Tricolor do *not* fly with the many other national flags near the base of de Lesseps' statue, but the welcome we received could not have been more friendly. However, the Port Said Military Museum contains a panorama and several large paintings depicting our complete destruction, and it seemed better to keep a low profile while these were being proudly shown to a large party of school children. Perhaps their lives are going to be less eventful than ours, but in 1996 it seems unlikely. The only absolute certainty is that the Airborne Forces Security Fund will prove an essential support to the old and bold who were our comrades—many of them not old at all but invalided early in life. They, and more particularly their families, will deserve help well into the next millenium.

Chapter I

WINGS OF THE MORNING

'RED on. Stand in the door!'

Sergeant Crompton edged forward. The slipstream tore at his smock. The aircraft wheeled slowly towards the rising sun and the grey sea and ochre sand-bars of the Egyptian coast rolled below the starboard wing. On November 5th, 1956 we were running in to Port Said.

The parachutists behind me packed up close, and I was squeezed aft towards the doorway. The compression increased until all twenty of us in the stick were jammed tight. 'Stick' denotes the number of men jumping from an aircraft in any particular drop. At the back of the stick the boys had a vested interest in cramming us tighter still. In less than five minutes they expected to be fighting for their lives.

We waited a long time. Fatigue and tension mounted. Each of us was carrying about a hundred and twenty pounds of equipment and we all knew that everything depended on jumping quickly and regularly at the rate of one man per second. Nothing must go wrong. Any delay would mean disaster. El Gamil airfield, our Dropping Zone, was just long enough to take a stick of twenty men. And machine-gun posts covered both ends.

This, then, was what all that training had been for. How the mind rambles. Pack a little closer. Damned hot. Shindy in Parliament. Eden. Red light. Watch the strop of the man in front. Red still. What the *hell* am I doing here?

*   *   *

The mocking incredulous voice at breakfast eleven months (or was it years?) ago.

'My dear chap, you should have your head examined.'

At St. Thomas's Hospital the resident staff live in College House. Breakfast is a sepulchral meal, most of the residents being short of sleep. Conversation is limited to bleary and laconic shop. My time as a house-surgeon was drawing to a close and National Service loomed ahead. I had just wondered aloud whether to sign on for three years in the Royal Army Medical Corps, instead of the compulsory two.

The Resident Assistant Surgeon, who acted as our mentor, continued witheringly:

'Whatever for? Army medicine is nothing but dustbins and smelly feet.'

But it had been tempting. Barbara and I were about to get married. Pay and married quarters favoured those on a 3-year engagement. And a year spent in the wards and corridors and operating theatres of the great hospital had left one ready for a change.

So a week later I went for an interview at the War Office and persuaded the powers-that-be that I was an enthusiastic recruit. I was accepted for three years. The Director General Army Medical Services cryptically brought things to a close.

'Well I expect we'll manage to send you down the river before long.'

This was in answer to my statement that I would welcome service abroad.

He did not, however, specify the Nile.

*   *   *

Even then I would not have finished up in the number 17 position of 'Chalk 7'. (On operations chalk numbers are scrawled on the fuselage of each aircraft to simplify loading and marshalling.) I would not have been Regimental Medical Officer to 3 PARA, as the 3rd Battalion the Parachute Regiment is generally called. If I now found myself taking part in a shattering piece of gunboat-diplomacy which I deplored, I had no one to blame except myself. And David Hartley.

16

David had been a contemporary at St. Thomas's and a good friend. His tall angular frame, supporting a huge grin, receding fair hair, and thick horn-rimmed glasses was a welcome sight at Waterloo station. The mild blue eyes lit up when it transpired that we were called up on the same day. David had just become an enthusiastic rock-climber. His irrepressible sense of humour had lightened several rain-soaked afternoons in the gullies of North Wales. The chance of climbing again together was encouraging.

'Bet we spend the whole blooming time in Aldershot,' he had said, as the train whirled us away. So we had spent the journey devising means of escape from this humdrum fate.

It had been a roundabout journey from the Aldershot train to the Valetta transport aircraft approaching Port Said. At that time the Army attempted the heroic and impossible task of converting newly recruited doctors into officers and gentlemen in the space of a fortnight. At the Royal Army Medical Corps depot at Crookham a whirlwind series of lectures covered, in theory, every aspect of military administration. Meanwhile patient instructors taught us the elements of drill, saluting and even a little weapon training. It was during this time that we received a lecture from Lieutenant-Colonel Kilgour who commanded the 23rd Parachute Field Ambulance. Speaking very quietly, with the slightest impediment in his speech he explained the nature and purpose of his unit. (He was, he said frankly, recruiting.) In the mildest and most insidious way he pointed out the advantages of serving with the Parachute Brigade. His loyalty to his own Corps prevented him from more than hinting at the risks of 'dustbins and smelly feet' inherent in serving anywhere else. To end the lecture he produced a member of his Field Ambulance fully equipped for jumping. There, he implied, with a few months training, went we.

A brief whispered conversation and David and I both volunteered. Three weeks later I was handed a telegram.

'Report Maida Barracks Aldershot Monday April 23rd for Airborne Training.'

This was the Parachute Selection or 'P' course. The atmosphere at Maida Barracks was different. The buildings were just the same as any other barracks; the same cracked tarmac separated the shabby slate-roofed barrack blocks. But the men were unlike soldiers I had seen elsewhere.

They all marched fast. And noticed things at great distances. I picked my way uncertainly towards the 'P' Company office, and found myself returning salutes at a range of anything up to a hundred yards. As I barely knew how to salute myself, I was relieved to reach cover in the office building. I was ushered into the Company Commander.

Genial scrutiny was the first impression of Harry Thompson. As Major in charge of 'P' Company he had to decide in the space of two weeks whether about a hundred and twenty officers and other ranks should be accepted by the Brigade for parachute training. He wasted no time. From the moment we shook hands I knew I was on probation. A few searching questions laid bare my activities of the past ten years.

'Well, doc, we don't expect you to be fit. But we do want to see you have a go.'

His florid countenance wrinkled into the suspicion of a grin, and the ginger moustache twitched with concealed humour. I saluted and went out.

The colour sergeant issued me with denim overalls and a parachutist's helmet. This felt surprisingly heavy on the head.

Next morning we paraded at 8 a.m. The men fell in in squads of thirty, and the officers a few yards to the rear. Names were called. Each man had a number chalked on his trouser pocket and helmet. The few officers were spared this indignity. Nevertheless, it made one feel like a political prisoner, standing drab and helmeted in the early sunshine.

That had been my first meeting with Sergeant Crompton. He had been gruff on 'P' course. An enthusiastic boxer, the long years of training had left him in a state of chronic fitness.

'P' course was designed not so much to test fitness as mental stamina or determination. The technique was simple. Make everyone tired, and then get them to do something they dislike or are normally afraid of. Repeat this daily for ten days, and towards the end of the second week the potential parachutists can be picked out fairly easily.

To get tired, we ran. In boots the squad crunched at the double out of barracks and along those endless straight avenues. A diversion over the tank tracks in Long Valley returned us muddy and shambling to the hard straight road. Then uphill back to barracks.

'Squad, halt!' One, one-two. The crunch stopped.

A few minutes' pause, and into the huge Maida gymnasium for P.T. and 'milling'. During milling two men of equal weight and wearing boxing gloves were put into a ring and left to knock hell out of each other for two minutes.

I had nearly been driven into the ground in the first few blows. That was not the point. You had to show you could take it if you were unable to give it.

After this the swimming bath sounded like light entertainment. The squad fell in on the parade ground and doubled half a mile down Queen's Avenue to the baths. It was bathing with a difference. One at a time we mounted the 15-foot diving board and on the command 'Go!' jumped in. Non-swimmers were fished out as soon as they surfaced. 'Go!' again the swimmers somersaulted in backwards.

Lunch in the Mess, where the 'P' course candidates sat awkwardly apart from their examiners. When you are tired enough appetite vanishes. Then back to the 'Trainasium', an area of beechwoods bedecked with cables, platforms, scrambling nets and scaffolding.

'Go!' and you jumped a five-foot gap in platforms twenty feet above the ground. 'Go!' and you cast loose on a pulley sixty feet up to slither down a cable. 'Go!' and you jumped for the rope which, if you caught it, would swing you over the ten foot gap between the branches.

19

'Go!' and you jumped. . . . Simple, applied Pavlov. The conditioned reflex. Dogs can learn tricks. Soldiers can learn to jump.

We jumped, and at the same time we absorbed a little of what had gone before us. Though traditions make a good whipping post, a music hall joke, none of us on 'P' course felt tempted to make fun of the traditions of the Brigade we hoped to join. One quiet afternoon we were shown *Theirs is the Glory* —the film of Arnhem. The fact that several of our instructors had survived the battle made it uncomfortably real to us. Youth is an imaginative time, and brave failure stirs one deeper than success or victory. History books from Thermopylae onwards are full of brave failures. The crowd filing out of the lecture room after the film was unwontedly subdued.

Two of my brothers-in-law had been at Arnhem. Paddy as a gunner had been taken prisoner, escaped and swam the Rhine. Rob, despatching parachute troops with Transport Command, had been lucky to get home in a riddled Dakota. Both of them had lost many friends there. So perhaps I was more subdued than most.

On 'P' course we had learnt little about the technique of parachuting, save how to react to the command 'Go!' The fortnight at Maida Barracks passed with agonising slowness. Our bruises became more numerous, and faces assumed the greyness of men pushed near their limit. On an assault course I dropped a twelve foot log onto my toe. The nail separated and had to be removed by the depot Medical Officer. It looked like the end of 'P' course for me.

Gloomily I retired to the bedroom in barracks. This I shared with a young Sapper officer, Graham Owens. Graham had the build and stamina of a good second-row Rugby forward. He seemed the ideal man to sail through 'P' course with no trouble at all.

Graham lay on his bed dourly surveying the bruises on his shins. We had spent any spare time during the last few days doing just this.

'Reckon I've had it now.' I explained the toenail.

'They'd never fail you on that. I got a rocket from the Company Commander this morning. That's my lot.'

Graham was clearly depressed beneath his normally composed and bluff exterior. The prospect of failure, or even worse, a 're-course' making one go through the whole thing again was dismal. But two days later we were informed that about half the course had passed, and to our surprise Graham and I were among them.

The survivors of 'P' course reassembled at Abingdon three days later for the parachute course. I had felt iller than my bruises merited during the last few days at Aldershot. Learning to roll on the floor in the big training hangar was misery. I reported sick and was quickly diagnosed as having contracted glandular fever by the Station Medical Officer. This tiresome, inconclusive and rambling disease was to have repercussions.

There was a shortage of parachute-trained doctors when I fell sick at Abingdon. David Hartley was summoned from a hygiene course elsewhere and leap-frogged into my place. He completed his parachute training in a fortnight and flew out to Cyprus shortly afterwards to join '1 PARA', the first battalion, proudly wearing his Wings.

My return to Abingdon was circuitous. After convalescing for a month I rejoined the 23rd Parachute Field Ambulance in Aldershot. Here Lieutenant-Colonel John Kilgour managed to preserve the feeling that something was about to happen, however tedious our routine appeared. One would find him, 'just checking the Hastings loading tables', or 'looking up what we've got left in Mafraq'. The impression was given that if you too didn't know how much a four-engined Hastings transport aircraft would carry, or what medical stores remained in Jordan, you might live to regret it. This lent a pleasant urgency to our training which might otherwise have been very dull.

It had been a halcyon month with the 23rd Parachute Field Ambulance. We had lived in a collapsing old cottage, complete with collapsing old owner, on the outskirts of Farnham. Then at the end of July, Nasser nationalised the Suez Canal. John Kilgour's prognostications came true. Something had happened.

A great tide of Reservists returned to the Parachute Brigade. Every man had to be inoculated and medically examined, and the Field Ambulance worked late into the night. The Reservists had all fulfilled a three-year regular engagement and were on the Reserve for a further four years. With remarkable philosophy they cast off their civvy clothes and jobs, and found their way back into their old units.

Four days after the Canal had been nationalised we had set sail for Cyprus aboard H.M.S. *Theseus*. As the aircraft carrier threshed through the warm summer sea we all understood the politics perfectly. Nasser had grabbed the Canal. We were going to grab it back again.

For those who like sea voyages it had been pleasant. The days had been enlivened with lectures on Cyprus by those who knew the Island, and on hygiene and first aid by the doctors. We had practised with Sten guns and pistols over the stern, hoping at least to achieve safety with our friends if not certain death to our enemies in the process. These modest hopes were later both to be dashed. The assembly on board was a motley crowd: the gunner regiment of the Brigade, the Field Ambulance, Ordnance, Sapper and Workshop units, about two thousand men in all. Before leaving Portsmouth we had been assembled on the flight deck for an address by the Brigadier. The deck itself was covered with 3-ton lorries, ambulances, 'Champs' and their trailers lashed into position in neat rows. Brigadier M. A. H. Butler, D.S.O., M.C. selected a heap of baggage as his rostrum. Everyone crowded round: an address from 'Tubby' Butler was something of a rarity.

The neat light figure, red beret at a just-off-rakish angle climbed quickly to the top of the pile of tents, poles and tarpaulins, and caught one foot in a loose wire.

'Watch it,' said a voice from the crowd. Tubby looked

doubtfully at his platform and spoke into the Tannoy microphone.

'This is my *first* hazard,' he said. 'But Nasser has done in a week what I've been trying to do for six months. He's got my B rigade together again.'

'Good old Nasser,' said another voice.

Since January 1956 the Brigade had been divided. Two b attalions, the First and Third, had been sent to Cyprus ready to take action in Jordan if necessary. Glubb Pasha had just b een sacked by King Hussein and trouble seemed likely. The S econd Battalion had moved to Cyprus in June. Now the remainder of the Brigade was following.

Hands on hips Tubby had continued. He rapidly told us about 'these EOKA characters' and 'this bloke Grivas'. He ended with a brief tirade about safety: 'We've had too many blooming shooting accidents as it is.' And discipline. 'If you don't salute my vehicle I'll put you on a charge. Not because I like being saluted, but because you *must* be alert.' His racy, cheerful manner held everyone. Long afterwards his words stuck in my mind. A later harangue ended typically: 'Mind you I'm not saying it can't be fun. If you really don't enjoy your soldiering you might as well give up and buy a bloody sweetshop.'

A mere five days after leaving Portsmouth H.M.S. *Theseus* had anchored off Famagusta on the east coast of Cyprus. The laborious transfer of vehicles, baggage and ammunition into lighters had begun. It seemed surprising that in eighty-odd years of colonial rule Britain had not managed to construct a deep-water harbour. Had she done so the Island's economy would have benefited enormously. But again and again we were to see the harvest which these lost opportunities had reaped. Much good had been done on the Island, but parsimony or laissez-faire caused much to be neglected or postponed. More money and more energy expended peacefully a few years ago might have forestalled the enormous expense and tragedy of EOKA.

As darkness fell a smart explosion under the ship reminded us that EOKA existed. The Captain appeared at once on the quarterdeck and asked what was going on. It transpired that the Commander, suspecting a frogman below, had dropped a grenade over the side. He had won the V.C. in a midget submarine, attacking a German pocket battleship, and could be expected to know the potentialities of frogmen.

Our subsequent alarms were not always so false.

We went ashore and drove in open lorries through the blazing morning heat to Nicosia. John Kilgour took me on one side.

'I've just been on the telephone to the 3rd Battalion adjutant. You're to join them tomorrow. They've not had a Medical Officer now for a month.'

So we had driven next day round the old city of Nicosia to Tunisia Camp, perched on an arid escarpment alongside the airfield. Here I had met '3 PARA'.

John Kilgour had introduced me to Captain Gerald Mullins, the adjutant, and left. I felt like a new boy abandoned at school. Gerald explained the situation. The battalion was flying home for airborne training which could not be provided in Cyprus. Gerald was hard pressed, as the Air Adjutant had flown home with the earlier aircraft, and he was having to organise departures. Despite numerous telephone calls, and runners who appeared every few minutes with messages, he took great care to explain the details of my next moves. The tent was hot and dusty, frequent distracting messages were brought in by runners, but Gerald at work was unflappable. His generous frame belied an agile mind, and he could produce astonishing bursts of speed on the rugger field. A runner was summoned.

'Go and fetch Corporal Dunbavin from the medical tent.'

A few minutes later the Corporal had arrived and saluted smartly. He was dressed in a red beret, blue shorts and boots. Close-cropped fair hair showed at his neck. I was taken in at a glance. The new boss arriving. Without wings on my sleeve I felt naked.

'Yessir.'

I was introduced.

'Show the Medical Officer around.'

And we had gone to see the dust-floored sixteen by sixteen foot tent which was to be my office. The medical orderlies were called to attention and I tried to memorise their names. All wore the same shorts and boots only. Stringy brown limbs and torsos. Six of them sizing me up. This was my empire.

The Corporal obviously knew his stuff. A true East Anglian, he had joined the army as a boy and spent several years in the Drums Platoon. He was the most experienced soldier among the orderlies and was frequently to be heard arguing points of the battalion's recent history with the medical Sergeant. His repertoire of 'Rock' songs was huge, rivalled only by his capacity for producing nauseating puns to order.

'I'm just off to do Grivas bodily harm'—and the Corporal took his pistol down to the range. 'Only you can make this change in me!'—sung fortissimo, and the Corporal straightened his beret to go on parade. He had acquired a fair mastery of the working of the medical side of his job and the military problems too. The Sergeant and he between them had steered me through the various perils which beset a newly joined Medical Officer. They knew most of the battalion, Reservists included, by name and livened sick parade with pithy asides. Gradually I learnt a lot that no formal course of instruction could have taught.

And I got to know 3 PARA.

CHAPTER II

'EIGHT HUNDRED FEET. FIVE MEN JUMPING'

FOUR days after arriving in Cyprus on H.M.S. *Theseus* I had flown home with 3 PARA. The battalion was brushing up its airborne training. The Medical Officer did not know how to jump at all.

The airborne training in which the battalion was to take part was primarily for the benefit of the Royal Air Force. Comparatively few of the Transport Command pilots had recent experience of dropping parachutists. We did not know this.

But at Abingdon it was all different. *Knowledge dispels fear* is the laconic motto of the Parachute Training School. The whole programme is aimed at passing on knowledge and experience quickly and efficiently. Since the early days at Ringway during the war the Royal Air Force has been responsible for the training of parachutists. Various courses now run simultaneously. The regular soldiers spend a month over their eight descents. The Territorials compress them into a fortnight. I found myself being directed from squad to squad in order to get it all over in time to return to Cyprus with 3 PARA.

The first morning was bad. It was a Sunday and everyone seemed to be away for the week-end. With a Parachute Jumping Instructor who had clearly had a good party the night before I did 'synthetic' solo. For synthetic training a hangar converted into a vast gymnasium is used. There are mock-up fuselages of various aircraft, swings, pulleys, shutes and innumerable large mats cover most of the floor space. On these you roll.

I practised rolling forward left, forward right, backward left, backward right, side left, side right. . . .

'Feet and knees together, sir.' Thump! On the shoulder. 'Shoulders a little more rounded next time, sir.' Crash! On the back of my head. 'Tuck the chin in now, sir.' After half an hour of this my headache must have made the Sergeant's seem trivial. Normally in a squad one had a rest between crashes, but this solo tuition was continuous. We had progressed to shutes and swings, practising landings. Then 'exits' from a dummy fuselage. 'Flight' from a swinging parachute harness. Finally the 'fan'.

The 'fan' was reputed to be the nearest approach to the real thing which the hangar provided. We climbed up about 25 feet to a platform. The floor looked a long way below. A sketchy harness was attached by a thin wire to a revolving drum on the spindle of a small fan. As you jumped the wire unreeled from the drum and the revolving fan braked your descent.

I had been glad eventually to leave the hangar that Sunday at Abingdon. The first balloon jump was fixed up for five-thirty next morning. It seemed a good idea to get away from it all for a few hours. Barbara and a friend had to be driven over to Hindhead and I got away with such success that it was 1 a.m. before I went to bed.

So when we were woken at four my emotions were blunted by tiredness.

The horrors of 'ballooning' had often been described to me. To some extent I was prepared for the gamut of feelings to which it subjects the jumper. Parachuting is the ideal pastime for those who enjoy contrasts. For in a very short time you can experience successively fatigue, boredom, apprehension, fear, beauty, pain and exhilaration. And finally a complete physical and emotional exhaustion which is satisfactory in itself. The very speed with which these feelings pass engraves them indelibly on the fading tablets of memory. I imagine only drowning or approaching the gallows can rival, and for a shorter time, this intensity of experience. Indeed to the novice parachutist the sensation of impending death seems comparable with either of these.

'You're not afraid of jumping, only of refusing to jump,' Colonel Kilgour had said to us that morning at Crookham. That might be. As the balloon lifted unsteadily from the dew-spangled grass—how green and moist after Cyprus—jumping seemed equally terrible. But refusing would be ignominious.

'Eight hundred feet. Five men jumping.'

The instructions were called out casually by the Royal Air Force despatcher to the crew manning the winch lorry. I felt anything but casual. I was one of the five.

Everything happened as prophesied. The false bonhomie we had adopted among us faded as the cable was paid out. At two hundred feet the figures on the ground became just blotches of pale faces looking up at us. Five hundred feet and silence descended, broken only by encouraging chatter from the sergeant who was to despatch us.

'Lovely day for your first, sir.' And it was. The low bright sunlight silhouetted the folds in the gentle water meadows, and threw long shadows from the heavy clumps of trees. Mist shrouded the Thames. Somewhere underneath it was Abingdon Lasher, the weir which, ages ago, had terminated the agony of our weekly 'lock-to-lock' courses. Rowing a four miles 'lock-to-lock' would be paradise compared with this.

Our upward movement stopped and the balloon cage settled with an ominous slope downhill towards the doorway, which was protected by a flimsy wooden bar. One seemed all too likely to fall out, let alone jumping.

'When I get the blue flag from the ground I shall start,' said the despatcher as he freed the bar. The unprotected void dragged at us. Craning over the side I saw a yellow flag waving from side to side. Thank God, we might yet be postponed or cancelled.

'Okay. There's the blue.' Last hope gone.

'Stand in the door, number one.' Charles Hemming, a subaltern in the Essex Regiment who was doing the course for the fun of the thing (what fun?), made ready in the doorway. The despatcher gave the attachment of his static line to the strong point overhead a last knowing feel. How I loved him for that final kind gesture. I moved round as number two and Sapper Sowerby was number three behind me. I shall never forget those positions.

'Go!' Charles was despatched. The jerking snap of metal and webbing as his static line paid out was like the crack of doom. I shuffled into position and took a despairing downward glance. His parachute appeared to have opened. The despatcher should have been a psychiatrist.

'Hand just a little further round the door, sir,' in a confidential whisper; 'chest out, sir, and look your own height. Very good position, sir.' I seemed to be leaning over backwards. David Hartley told me that at this moment on his first jump he decided to give it all up and take up market gardening.

'Go!' An enormous shout into my left ear from a distance of six inches. I was so surprised that I went.

The nauseating 'ugh' of falling lasted till I realised what was happening. A great hissing of wind in my chin-strap and clothes spoke of unchecked speed. I gradually slipped backwards with my feet rising to the horizon. The fall hurtled on and I lay supine on nothing except a lot of fading hope. Of course the damn thing wasn't going to work. I'd always known it wouldn't. When should I pull the reserve? 'Seven seconds till you hit the ground.' Surely ten had passed. The sun shone on my boots. At least it was a comfortable way of dying, just plummeting into the ground. I should feel nothing.

But something *was* happening behind me. Little staccato plucks at my back as the ties broke one by one and then a whoosh of deceleration. I looked up and saw the great silky jellyfish of fabric open and breathe. Lovely, marvellous thing. Veined with the seams and dappled flutings of its panels. Khaki and olive green shadows.

It had worked!

But I should be doing something. 'Look at the ground and assess your drift.' Flat welcoming grass sliding towards me. Just pull down slowly on the back lift webs and correct that. Wonderful. Now those feet and knees and shoulders and elbows. Keep the chin down whatever happens. This is terrific, just as they said. But the ground has speeded up and is going the other way now. Blades of grass.

'BLOODY HELL!' The despairing tones of the instructor through the loud-hailer. Thump-bump-crash, as feet, bottom and helmet hit the ground in quick succession.

It appeared that I should have let up on the lift-webs to avoid cannoning in backwards. The instructor was brief and to the point. He had been shouting himself hoarse for some time as I came down. The haze of gratitude and self-admiration in which I had been basking up there had masked all that. But I'd made it.

And for about ten seconds I had been God.

It was humiliating to find that I didn't know how to roll up the parachute. The remainder of the squad had learnt this during the previous week, but my morning in the hangar had not gone beyond the bare essentials of reaching the ground safely. I had just finished tying the bag up to enclose the enormous area of nylon canopy.

'Report back to the parachute store,' said the instructor, 'there's an aircraft taking off in fifteen minutes.'

So I drew another parachute and fitted it, and climbed with a stick of twenty men into a Valetta. Our instructor emplaned last.

'I shall jump first,' he said. 'But don't copy my exit. Concentrate on your own.'

You would think that getting out of the large doorway of an aircraft is all too easy. It would be, but for the slipstream. The aircraft is flying at 100 knots and the propellers are clawing air at twice this speed past the fuselage. So when you jump, it is into a gale of 200 m.p.h. The problem is to burst quickly and neatly from the sheltered enclosure of the aircraft into this torrent of air. If you step out slowly you start to twist like a top and your parachute rigging lines are twisted also. If you are slower still your head may be thumped against the fuselage as you fall down outside it, or you may receive a 'strop-burn' from the webbing strops of the previous jumpers. These hang flailing in the slipstream as each parachute opens, and are all retrieved by the despatcher after the stick has gone. The instructors, jumping unladen and by themselves, solved the 'exit' problem by running full tilt across the whole width of the aircraft and straight out of the door.

My own exit was timid enough. But I can still feel that giant breath of warm air, and see the silver sword of the tailplane flash overhead.

For each of my eight jumps had been equally vivid. Outstanding was the third. We were back in the balloon in the early morning and the certainty of the long unchecked drop weighed heavily on all of us.

The fourth was gusty. The wind was getting up as we took off from Abingdon and the rate of my drift across the airfield at Weston-on-the-Green was frightening. I got it under some sort of control and then, thirty feet up, the canopy blasted away to one side. I was in for an awful smash. In pure cowardice I assumed a sort of foetal position, looking like the 'hear no evil' monkey. Thump and clang, clang, clang as my helmet hit the ground in three rapid somersaults. Such was my relief and confusion that I pulled the reserve parachute in my efforts to get out of the harness. More ignominy.

I suppose with experience and greater skill I should eventually have been able to control or predict my landings. In the event, it was usually a case of making the best of a bad job at the last possible moment. The force was so varied. It could be like jumping off a stationary low table or from a train, backwards, at thirty miles an hour. Until the last fraction of a second I never knew which to expect.

The night jump was the most dramatic. We went from a Hastings in short sticks of three. The aircraft gradually

31

emptied. The lights were dimmed and the Red and Green tremendously bright by contrast. The empty blackness outside the doorway and the difficulty in seeing what one was doing all heightened the tension and anticipation. Each little stick seemed to have jumped straight into oblivion. It was almost an anticlimax to meet up again afterwards. The actual descent was a constant debate with myself about the closeness of the ground, which nevertheless took me by surprise. My landing was more 'like a sack of spuds' than usual. Next day two jumps with equipment had ended the course at Abingdon.

While I was learning to jump the battalion had not been idle. But with a consideration for his soldiers which I later came to expect, the Colonel insisted that every man should have the maximum possible amount of leave during the short stay in England. Some exciting airborne training, flown by the unpractised pilots, took place. Frensham Dropping Zone, which they used, was a narrow strip of common between a small lake and a pinewood. Many members of the battalion were able to brush up their technique for landing in water or in trees. After a few days of this everyone was sent on leave, with the promise to be back for a battalion exercise three days later.

Not a man was late.

I saw them arrive at Abingdon for the exercise. The battalion was to jump on the desolate, sad Imber Dropping Zone on Salisbury Plain. From the slopes above you can see the ruined village nestling forlornly in its shattered elm trees. Since the war the village has been used for street-fighting practice. Only the church is inviolate. It feels haunted.

The prospect of jumping in such a depressing spot did not seem to deter them. Nor did the infuriating delay which they had to endure while the weather cleared. Parachuting makes you take the word meteorologist philosophically. To prophesy the velocity of the wind within five knots must be very difficult. But to a parachutist it is vital. With wind speeds up to fifteen knots jumping is safe. Above this speed the injury rate on landing rises alarmingly.

At last the Battalion exercise had been 'on'. I watched the long lines of men pick up their weapon-containers from the hangar. Every man wore a faded smock with tell-tale green flashes on the sleeves. A feeling of scruffy efficiency prevailed. They climbed into three-ton trucks and drove round the perimeter track to the waiting aircraft. Coughing engines sent puffs of blue smoke into the afternoon as the line of Hastings and Valettas were marshalled into order. The clear air was vibrant with the open roar as each pilot warmed his engines for take-off. In pairs the aircraft sped down the runway and curled flatly round to starboard above the woods of Boar's Hill. Looking brave and defiant they headed for Salisbury Plain against a lowering backcloth of cumulo-nimbus clouds.

After Abingdon there had been a few days of exquisite leave. The knowledge that it was short, and the uncertainty of when there would be any more, made it poignant. Then a rainy afternoon found me on an open lorry, driving to Blackbushe airfield near Aldershot. I was surrounded by soldiers in bleached red berets.

The battalion was returning to Cyprus.

From then onwards I had continually been meeting new faces. New ranks, new units, new sub-units, abbreviations, procedures, weapons, plans, drills, ceremonies. It had all been to me a magnificent military confusion. Gradually, over the weeks I had achieved a sketchy idea of what composed a Parachute Battalion and how it all worked. I had learned slowly.

At Blackbushe I was introduced to Major Walsh who commanded 'A' Company of the battalion. Mike Walsh was about twenty-eight at the time, and I knew from David Hartley that he had narrowly escaped being killed in a forest fire which had broken out on one of the anti-EOKA operations in Cyprus. It was hard to believe that this gentle-eyed young man with receding hair had endured all that. He and his wife Angela were having one of those miserable last minute cups of tea which all soldiers' wives somehow accept as routine. Most

33

kindly, for I was an absolute 'gooseberry', they invited me to join them. Later we boarded a Hermes airliner and flew in comfort back through the night. Mike made very light of his own troubles as the long hours droned by.

But I heard a good deal of what had gone before.

It was all a huge mistake. Not only the political situation in Cyprus, but the very presence there of the Parachute battalions. Cyprus was not primarily their pigeon. Early in the year the 1st and 3rd Battalions had flown out from England to be held ready to drop in Jordan. 'British lives and Property,' those unfortunate and recurrent chestnuts, were once more in jeopardy. But the Jordan alarm had fizzled out. It would have been logical for the battalions to return home. As units of the Strategic Reserve, depending on home resources for their maintenance and training, they could more rapidly be re-deployed from England. Our recent return home emphasised this. Doubtless they would in fact have flown home again. But for EOKA.

The long-standing agitation for Enosis, or union of Cyprus with Greece, had finally flowered into a vicious terrorist campaign. In 1954 Colonel Grivas had come secretly to Cyprus from Athens to direct operations personally. This embittered, regular soldier was at last having his fling. The fact that his army largely consisted of schoolchildren, priests and irresponsible youths did not worry him. He had not received the recognition he felt that he deserved for his part in the war against the Germans. At the end of the war, when Greece was threatened by Communism, he had fought desperately with the extreme right-wing faction in Athens. During savage street-fighting the Communists had only been beaten finally by the intervention of the British 2nd Parachute Brigade. It was one of the fine ironies of Middle Eastern politics that some of the men who had saved him then were now asked to hunt him down.

His campaign of civil disobedience, bomb-throwing, and murder had succeeded. The schoolchildren and youths had brought more attention from the British Government in twenty months than the diplomats had achieved in the previous twenty years. At last Grivas had arrived. During the spring of 1956 terrorist outrages had reached a new peak of ferocity. The Governor of Cyprus, General Sir John Harding, asked for the Parachute battalions to stay to combat EOKA.

So they had remained in the Island. Throughout the hot, dry summer they had mounted one anti-EOKA, or 'Internal Security' operation after another. Some had met with more success than others. I was to hear more of these later.

CHAPTER III

THE SPIRIT OF THE WARRIOR

WE had walked out of the Hermes onto the tarmac of Nicosia airfield. The gasping heat of Cyprus noon had us out of our smocks in no time. Lovely rain it had been at Blackbushe.

The trouble with overnight travel is the disorientation in time which it produces. We had returned to Tunisia Camp and sought shelter in the officers' mess tent. I must make some attempt to grasp who was who. Numerous figures lounged around in bizarre combinations of mufti and uniform. Knowing the regiment had a reputation for unorthodoxy I dressed in sympathy for several days afterwards. I had not realised that our dazed and superheated arrival was on a Sunday. If possible the Colonel arranged that the Sabbath was a military *dies non*. Lawrence Scragg, the major who commanded 'Headquarter' Company, had gently pointed out the error of my ways.

Lawrence might well have been a martinet, but his sense of humour saved him. He often pretended to be one, giving orders of questionable necessity which he expected to be obeyed without question. I later found that a direct stare and a murmured protest would produce, as often as not, a crease at the corner of the mouth and a twinkle in the eye.

'Okay, doc, perhaps not this time, then,' and I would escape some appalling chore, like examining the twenty pairs of Drummers' feet, or going round all the Deep Trench latrines to write up my 'Hygiene Diary'.

Lawrence's attitude to doctors had been partly conditioned by Basil, my predecessor. He and Lawrence had undergone several differences of opinion, until, in one excellent party, the Medical Staff had celebrated something or other rather too riotously even for 3 PARA. At present Basil was acting as Medical Officer to the gunners.

From Lawrence I had inherited Holden, my batman. Holden had just returned to the battalion as a Reservist. Phlegmatically he had abandoned the job of navvying among the Sussex downs, at which he earned up to seventeen pounds a week. For very much less pay he now looked after my clothes and my safety. He assumed, rightly, that as a soldier I was a dead loss, if not an actual menace. He would accompany me with a loaded rifle if he thought circumstances merited it.

Holden's navvying came into its own whenever during training we had been ordered to 'dig in'. Opening up a small slit trench in the shaly soil of Cyprus was an exhausting business. But his huge arms and shoulders tore the ground apart solidly, methodically. The vowel sounds of Sussex are round ones. Holden swearing, and he always did, was memorable. He had a great repertoire of unprintable songs and was in much demand whenever a sing-song took place.

Confusion of purpose is the outstanding memory of those first few weeks with 3 PARA. I had to learn how to deport myself as a member of the officers' mess, and pick up what I could about running the medical set-up. In camp we were based on the Medical Inspection or M.I. Tent: when the battalion was in the field we became known as the Regimental Aid Post or R.A.P.

Preparations for war were our immediate concern. So was the routine of sick parade, and the provision of medical cover for companies training outside camp. From time to time we would all depart on an Internal Security operation to combat the ever present nuisance of EOKA, after which our preparations would begin again where we had left off.

Nobody seemed to know what was to happen next. The Colonel addressed the battalion a few days after we returned to Cyprus and told us as much as he could. For his soldiers mattered to Lieutenant Colonel Paul Crook, O.B.E., who commanded the battalion. He knew that he had the finest bunch of soldiers that he was ever likely to command. In their knowing, and infallible, way the soldiers also recognised that he wasn't a bad C.O. They would have done anything he asked of them.

On the football ground near his office he mounted a make-shift rostrum. Everybody gathered round.

'While we were home on leave I was lucky enough to hear Ted Heath and see Middlesex play at Lord's,' he began. Murmurs of 'Lucky basket' from somewhere in the crowd, and 'Keep silence!' barked by the Regimental Sergeant Major. He went on to explain the importance of team-work in soldiering. The easy similes went home. Jazz or 'Rock' and games were close to everyone's heart and he enjoyed both. He had spent time in New Orleans in the great jazz days and his enthusiasm for it was infectious—never more so than when at times of celebration he would, by general demand, lead the singing of *Frankie and Johnny* to fervent applause. Whatever was coming next would involve 3 PARA, he continued, and therefore we should all be involved in some hard training in the weeks ahead. In this we were not disappointed.

It was from my sergeant that I had learnt most of the immediate background of the Colonel, the officers and men of the battalion. Sergeant Rabet knew them all. He had been Medical Sergeant for many years, and his job brought him directly in contact with everyone. The running of sick parades, the maintenance of inoculation states, routine medical examinations, all these were things whose organisation I left entirely to him.

'I've arranged to jab "B" Company tomorrow,' he would say as we finished sick parade. And sure enough the company would duly appear, complete with pay-books for their typhoid inoculations. I only had to give the injections. The disheartening task of entering the details in every man's medical documents and pay book he took in his stride. Many General Practitioners would envy such efficient help. Our medical tent, which did duty for both surgery and office, was a distracting place. The floor was of dried mud. Under the pounding of many pairs of feet this became a quarter-of-an-inch of fine, cocoa coloured dust, which pervaded everything. The papers always wore a film of it, and on windy days our instruments appeared to have been sterilised in drinking chocolate.

But neither the dust, nor heat, nor the endless succession of problems which were brought to him, distracted the sergeant. He handled them all firmly. Dust could be swept out, and the floor oiled or watered. Heat could be overcome by removing clothes, and the sergeant could usually be found dressed only in basket-ball boots and a pair of blue shorts. Problems were, above all, not to bother the Medical Officer. Everyone from Cypriot latrine-men to Company Commanders would politely be told when I was available for sick parades. The fact that I was available all the time did not matter.

'Give 'em a chance and they'll never let you alone,' he said. So I stuck firmly to my routine hours and saw 'Special Sick' only when they came properly dressed, and carrying a sick report. Beneath an air of military nonchalance he hid many of the qualities of a fanatic. He was dedicated to fitness as weaker mortals may be to horse racing or women. A spare moment would find him organising a game of basketball, at which he was brilliant. He captained the battalion team in a fiery, Gallic manner. The sergeant had spent the war in his native Jersey, under German occupation. Probably it was in those frustrating boyhood days that he had accumulated the gigantic reserves of energy which swept him through the trials of army life as if it were all a long, unscrupulous game. Our numerous stores and indents for supplies were simplicity itself. Over the years the sergeant had managed to 'win' a duplicate of all our permanent equipment. He always indented for a little more than we needed 'just in case'.

Despite the fact that he had probably forgotten more about the army and the running of the Regimental Aid Post than I was ever likely to know, he always managed to give the impression that I was in charge. And, more surprisingly, that I

39

knew what I was doing. One of his finest achievements during those chaotic weeks was the blood grouping. Transfusion of blood has made more difference to surgery, particularly war surgery, than even the use of antibiotics. At John Kilgour's insistence we had arranged for about eighty per cent of the battalion to have their blood groups ascertained. The laboratory at the British Military Hospital in Nicosia had borne the brunt of the work. The sergeant had handled most of the organisation. All I had to do was stick needles into veins to obtain the samples. The lists of results duly returned, and these were transferred to the men's identity discs. The checking and double checking of all these were arranged by the sergeant. We hoped that we would be able to provide donors on the spot to transfuse the wounded.

When the battalion was in camp Headquarter Company was an enormous organisation containing more than two hundred men, thus contrasting with the rifle companies each of which held about one hundred. On operations many of the Headquarter Company personnel were posted out to other companies, leaving a comparatively small Battalion Headquarters staff and various nuclei of other departments under the immediate command of Lawrence Scragg.

There were several small empires like ours in Headquarter Company. Our closest associates were the Intelligence Section, who were usually to be found manning the Battalion Headquarters Airborne Shelter nearby when we were in the field. The Intelligence Section were responsible for collecting, verifying and dispersing information. Much of it was too secret to disperse. They worked in a hut whose walls were plastered with maps and photographs of EOKA wanted men. Some of the latter were significantly crossed out from time to time. The Intelligence Section was held together by Sergeant Sparvell in much the same way as the Regimental Aid Post was organised by Sergeant Rabet. Both men had similar unique positions and worked with one officer only. This suited their separate temperaments well. If Sergeant Rabet was at first sight a Gallic enthusiast, Sergeant Sparvell was an Anglo-Saxon cynic. Long years in his position made him view any information, from whatever source, with scepticism. Disbelief had become a part of him.

The lieutenant who acted as Intelligence Officer, Jim Burke, was not obviously a cynic, but was temperamentally well suited to his job. Jim had spent several years in the Merchant Navy before joining the Parachute Regiment and was older and considerably more mature in many ways than his fellow subalterns. An innate gamesmanship and relish for the aura of cloaks and daggers which surrounded his work, made him the ideal Intelligence Officer.

If the Intelligence Section constituted the brains of the battalion when it took to the field, the nervous system was represented by the Signals Platoon, who occupied a tent near ours in camp.

A signaller's life was not a happy one, I had often thought. The Signals Platoon was commanded by Captain Watson, whom I had met briefly in the harrowing 'P' course days when he was at Airborne Forces depot. Tony Watson did not let his job get him down. He could laugh off the most infuriating failures in the reach-me-down wirelesses which were standard signalling equipment at that time. His men spent most of their time charging batteries or repairing sets, whenever a pause in training or operations gave them a chance. Time and again I had sat in the Battalion Command post when we were in the field for one reason or another. The Adjutant or officer on duty sat near the wireless set. Amorphous crackling or high-pitched musical squeaks came through the earphones. The signaller, like a priest saying mass, droned on.

'Hullo call sign one. I say again, how do you hear me? Over.' Repeated at half-minute intervals. Finally in despair, 'Hello call sign one. Nothing heard. Out.' Tony would explain this as 'interference' or 'trouble with the ionosphere', and proceed to organise a complicated relay of messages through one of the audible stations.

Of equal importance in co-ordinating the Battalion movements was the Mechanised Transport or 'M.T.' Platoon,
commanded by Captain Dawnay. Originally I had lived in
terror of him, and scarcely dared ask for my 'Stretcher Champ'
which did duty for an ambulance. Richard Dawnay's task was,
if possible, more desperate than Tony Watson's with the
signallers. Richard had a platoon of drivers, and was assisted
by two sergeants and a corporal. The staff may have produced
problems, but these paled beside those of the vehicles. The
vehicles had been stockpiled in Cyprus for many years and
were unpredictable. In addition they were driven hard over
rough roads. The result was that a considerable fraction of
Richard's force was often out of order. He had a harrowing
time attempting to increase the workable residue. Accidents
took a steady toll of vehicles, and temporarily, of some of their
drivers. If Richard was harrowed, the 'Turk' took it in his
stride. Sergeant Turkiewicz had travelled a long road to join
3 PARA. Beginning in Poland early in the war, he had somehow
found his way to join the Free Polish Forces, and eventually
the British Army. Now he acted as Richard's chief whipper-in.
Whenever I required the stretcher champ, the Turk would
bellow 'Smith!' into the dusty, wired-off acre of Cyprus which
held the 'M.T.' Park.

From the recesses of a bonnet in the distance a grimy,
apologetic figure would appear. Smith, my driver, was used to
sudden summonses.

'Be ready in a minute, sir.' And in a flash, by straightening
his beret and a token wash he smartened up enough to satisfy
Richard's eagle eye. In a cloud of limestone dust we would
swish out of the camp. Smith and I had lived all our lives
about a mile apart on the outskirts of Worcester. It had been
an incongruous delight to us both to realise this, as he drove me
up into the mountains of Cyprus. He had a gift for failing to
show surprise or emotion in a crisis. A slow, wry smile would
catch the corner of his mouth when anything particularly funny
happened. Otherwise tragedy and disaster left him apparently

unmoved. This was excellent. His job brought him face to face with plenty of both. In the hot exhausting Cyprus afternoons we had regaled each other with reminiscences of the rainfall and greenery of Worcestershire.

Throughout the whole company each of us depended for supplies on the company store, presided over by Colour Sergeant Bradley. The company Colour Sergeant supplies his company with everything. His store for the company is a miniature replica of the Quartermaster's store for the battalion. Nothing must get lost from the store, or be issued without being signed for by the recipient. All Colour Sergeants are experts at conserving their kit.

The Colour Sergeant was a cheerful character. On operations against EOKA in the hills of Cyprus he was responsible for feeding the company. An appalling hammering on mess tins and a bellow of 'come and get it' from the Colour Sergeant would indicate that he had succeeded in brewing up. All Colour Sergeants answered eventually to the Regimental Quartermaster Sergeant, and the Quartermaster. Chippy Robinson, the first of these, and Bob Grainger the latter, were the most authentic veterans in the battalion. Bob had survived Arnhem, being wounded and left behind after the main withdrawal. He had lived for some weeks behind the German lines and undergone a series of hair-raising escapes from recapture. On one occasion he had imitated a lunatic as German troops passed by, which must have been a considerable feat of acting. Anyone less like a lunatic than Bob would be hard to imagine, though for lucid sanity Chippy rivalled him.

Chippy was a small, lightly built figure. Long years of soldiering in all climates had reduced the skin of his face to a surface of creased mahogany. He had been reared, successfully, in the school of thought which reckoned that in hot climates soldiers could be treated like camels: filled with water occasionally and left to freewheel through the desert for days on end on a thimbleful of fluid from time to time. My en-

treaties for increased fluid intake for any reason would fall on
stony ground.

'Never needed it in Peshawar,' said Chippy, to which I lacked
the knowledge and courage to make a satisfactory reply.

Because of his lightness Chippy's parachute landings were
thistledown affairs, he would still be drifting around the sky
when the rest of his 'stick' had landed. On the hockey field
he was a deadly opponent, and in training the epitome of
stamina: nothing tired him. He would, when things were bad,
roll an extra cigarette or two, but otherwise human weakness
seemed to pass him by.

At regular intervals I was supposed to do a 'Hygiene
Round', inspecting sanitation in the camp generally and
recording my findings in a diary which was passed on to all the
authorities concerned for comment and action, if necessary.
The monotony of it palled after a time—one latrine is very
much like another—but in the early days with 3 PARA it did
provide an excuse for meeting people on their home ground.
This was welcome, for my memory for names is abysmal.

With the sergeant to guide me I would start in the officers'
and sergeants' messes and wander round the remainder of
Headquarter Company lines. First past the Pay Office,
always a welcome port of call. Major Edwards, our paymaster,
known to his friends in the Mess as 'Ted the pay' could be
relied on to the minutest detail. The passing of the years
demanded that Ted, whose parachuting career had begun in the
uncertain war-time training school at Rawalpindi, should
soldier in a less active arm. So with great regret he had transferred from his parent regiment to the Royal Army Pay Corps.
Inactivity was not for Ted. Whenever Headquarter Company
made a jump Ted was sure to be there. Years later I saw him
after a terrible descent from a helicopter in which he had
somersaulted through his rigging lines. The bemused figure,
slightly concussed, but courteous to the last, apologised for
asking me to look at his tongue, which he had bitten. Courtesy
and conscientiousness were deep in Ted's make-up. He had a

complete mastery of the intricacies of army pay, and would take endless pains to explain them to you if you were in doubt. Next were the tents of the Band and Drums. 3 PARA was the only battalion to have its band in Cyprus. Each battalion had a platoon of drummers, whose primary task on operations was the defence of Battalion Headquarters.

It somehow typified the distraction of September that in the midst of our preparations the Band and Drums beat 'Retreat' one evening. This ceremony is usually given months of intensive preparation and rehearsal. 3 PARA did it apparently impromptu and perfectly.

The battalion, standing in lines along the big parade ground had watched. The officers and their guests sat in an enclosure, facing across the ground towards the airfield. It grew on you. Band and Drums appeared to a conventional military march, and marched and countermarched, splitting into their separate units. The Drums had played a series of Reels and Strathspeys, and the brittle, precise, contrasting rhythms were blotted up by the empty evening sky. Then all assembled at the flagstaff where the Regimental Flag drooped limp in the windless air. To the sad, cool notes of 'Retreat' from the buglers the flag slowly came down. A Hastings dragged itself heavily off the runway opposite and turned west into the sunset, heading for England. It seemed symbolic. Ourselves in Cyprus. The Empire. 'The Consul at Sunset.' All the flags coming down soon for good. The Bandmaster saluted the Colonel and asked permission to march off.

Beating of 'Retreat' was the occasion for celebration throughout the battalion. A cocktail party was held in the mess, after which Noel Hodgson suggested we should see how the corporals were getting on in the 'Corporals Club'. Noel, then a major, was acting as President of the Regimental Institute. The holder of this portentous title, usually abbreviated to 'P.R.I.', is in charge of welfare generally. The provision of apparatus for sports, recreation and non-military amenities is his job. Not, you might think, of great concern to a front line fighting unit. But hard-worked, hard-trained fit young men must relax. If relaxing means getting bored there will very soon be trouble, and if there is enough trouble the front line fighting unit becomes inefficient. Boredom is the enemy in camp, whatever else awaits outside.

Combating boredom was no new experience to Noel. He had spent many years in and out of the Parachute Brigade, and soldiered through Korea with his parent regiment, the Durham Light Infantry. He is the only man I know to have chartered a London Taxi with the one word 'Newcastle!' This was to be back in time for an early morning parade when the last train had gone. 'It cost twenty-seven quid but the expression on the driver's face was almost worth it.' His prematurely grey hair gave an illusion of seniority, but the young face beneath, and the mantle of Court Jester which he frequently adopted in the mess, belied it. He was an ardent devotee of the battalion and the brigade.

We found that the corporals were getting on very well indeed. It was a whale of a party, but marred by my precipitate removal to see a corporal in 'C' Company who had been accidentally shot in the foot while cleaning his rifle to go on guard.

'C' Company had endured a run of ill fortune, none of which could be attributed to any failure of command or organisation, rather the reverse: each incident had been an unpredictable individual failure. A soldier had coughed in a night ambush and Grivas had been warned off. The next day a volley fired at long range by a 'C' Company patrol had missed him. This accidental shooting now seemed the last straw to the company commander, Major Norman.

Ron Norman was the only member of the officers' mess whose experience could rival that of Bob Grainger or Chippy Robinson. His experience of parachutists had begun in Crete. There he had watched the Germans jump from hedge-hopping Junkers 52 aircraft. They were flying so low that many of the troops had fallen into the ground before their parachutes had a chance to open. But their enormous losses had been eclipsed by their success. Ron had taken both lessons to heart and was a fervent protagonist of the Parachute Brigade. At the same time he knew the risks of arriving by air on the battlefield better than most. He took great care of his men. I used to ask his advice about all sorts of details which were quite outside the orbit of a company commander. Ron would blink slowly and, after a pause, give a reasoned, careful, complete answer. Nothing was too absurd to merit a considered reply. I never heard him say a hard word about anyone. But this mildness was not to be confused with weakness, as the ribbons of the M.B.E. and M.C. on the left breast of his khaki drill jacket declared. There was a quality of tranquillity in Ron Norman which you do not often meet in professional soldiers. The various heartaches of promotion or command seemed to make no impression on him. His wife and family had much to do with this. Throughout all the chaos of moves and partings which constitute the family life of a regular soldier, Ron, Mary and their five delightful children had remained a completely happy and united family.

Characteristically the Colonel entrusted to Ron's company with its recent record of ill luck, the only chance of an airborne exercise in Cyprus.

For such was the shortage of transport aircraft at that time that only one company could be dropped by parachute after we returned to Cyprus.

A few days later we were woken at first light to provide medical cover on the Dropping Zone. The medical staff piled into the Stretcher Champ and Smith drove us out beyond the village of Yerolakkos to the west of the camp. With its whitewashed church the village sparkled like a jewel in the dull beige plain as the sun's first rays caught it. We drove on over the crumbly ochre waste of plough. The long flat shadows of early morning picked out the undulations and gullies. Smith and I sat in the Champ to one side. The Sergeant and Corporal were chatting nearby.

'There they are, sir,' said Smith.

The six Valettas swept low over the hills to the west. Silently, for a few seconds before their sound reached us. Slow, straight and level they flew towards us in pairs. The first pair at six hundred feet, the second at eight hundred, the third at a thousand. Like the morning flight of duck.

The first pair reached the sodium flare which marked the dropping point. Away plunged the containers from the wings. Brightly coloured parachutes, green, red, blue, flowered from each. But before they had fully developed the men were tumbling out. Each tiny figure shot like a torpedo into the wake of the aircraft, trying to follow it across the sky. The parachutes burst open within a second and halted them. In twenty seconds it was all over. The Valettas flew away into the sun and their sticks littered the sky. The minute men under their parachutes each lowered a weapon-container and came swinging and sliding down towards us. Just as they neared the ground the next pair of aircraft came over dropping their loads. You didn't know where to look. Whether to watch the parachute-canopies developing overhead or the men thumping and rolling into the plough alongside.

With one exception the 'C' Company exercise had gone smoothly. One of the big containers fully loaded for war, had fallen off the aircraft prematurely. This contained rocket-launcher bombs and other ammunition, a windfall which no EOKA gang could afford to ignore. A frenzied hunt disclosed it, lying undiscovered in the hills to the west, and it was conveyed safely back to camp.

The most impressive part of the company exercise had been the air support. A squadron of Royal Air Force Vampire aircraft were on call for ground attack. The small, flimsy-looking jet fighters with their matchstick-thin twin booms stole the show completely. They were not firing their guns or rockets, simply making simulated attacks on targets given to them by wireless. Dodging the telephone wires they skimmed over the swelling contours and swooped up into the echoing morning

48

distance to vanish into the haze. Moments later with a blare of noise they were back, diving onto the exact hillock or hollow indicated. We had seen more of this later on the Brigade Field Firing exercise. Hearing the instructions passed was eerie. The Air Contact Team officer sat by his wireless set.

'Ten o'clock. A small hut. Target one hundred yards left.'

Back came a young, amiable voice, thin over the distance. The pilot might be twenty miles away over the sea and five thousand feet up. He sounded clinical, detached.

'Ten o'clock. A small hut. Target one hundred yards left.'

Within two minutes the terrible whining crescendo of noise built up and the flight of three aircraft dived steeply to loose their rockets onto the exact spot. They were using dummy warheads, but the impact was fearful. And accurate. The few oil drums which were clustered in groups as targets lay twisted and scattered like wrecked cars.

It was only 'Support' Company of the battalion which could produce anything approaching this fire power. Support Company contained three platoons, of mortars, medium machine guns and anti-tank guns respectively: between them they were capable of more destruction than the rest of the battalion put together. They were experts. They were commanded by Geoff Norton, a major on detachment from the Middlesex Regiment; he gave a full rein to his three platoon commanders and they served him well. Before I had been with the battalion long I was able to see for myself when the brigade held a field-firing exercise.

In the dusty plain at the eastern end of the Island, backed by the arid rocks of the northern range, the 'battle' raged for a day. Live ammunition produced a vast, echoing symphony of noise. Movement, bombardment, attack, consolidation. Easy and flowing in the absence of an enemy.

The mortars ended the day with a shattering bombardment into a gully. One bomb fell short, not far from 'A' Company waiting to attack. Howls of execration: 'Put your something sights up, mate!' Eventually the 'battle' ended. Norman

Morley who commanded the mortars had one or two 'duds' to explode. Norman was a humorist. He derived as much delight from the dialogue of his Birmingham batman and a 'Brummy' mortarman friend, as he did from occasional sorties to the '*Gourmet*'. In the '*Gourmet*' restaurant on the outskirts of Nicosia the officers were wont sometimes to escape the tedium of mess food.

How Norman knew about 'duds' in all the din which had gone before I couldn't think. Apparently mortar officers count, almost subconsciously, every bomb that explodes. We drove forward to the target area. It seemed surprisingly intact, just like any other gully in Cyprus. But mortar bombs explode in a vicious, superficial manner. Most of the force splatters out sideways. One unexploded bomb was obvious and easily lifted out of its shallow hole. The other was deeper. Norman scrabbled the shale away with his hands and the fins appeared. More digging was impossible. The ground was too hard.

'It's most unlikely to go off,' said Norman as he began to rock it out, wrenching gently to and fro on the fins. We sighed inaudibly as it came free. Norman laid it reverently with its fellow. A few Cypriots had emerged like coneys from the landscape and were scouring the area for copper scraps.

'Get those beggars away,' Norman said as he placed the slab of gun cotton beside the bombs. They were shooed unceremoniously behind a hillock. We rejoined Norman.

'Behind that hump will do,' said Norman. We cowered behind the mud bank. It seemed very small. He lit the fuse and walked with maddening deliberation back towards us. Etiquette demands this. To run is to admit you haven't cut enough fuse. A long wait, and then our ear-drums flapped with the force of the explosion. Splinters sang overhead and quiet returned to the plain.

The machine gunners displayed an easy familiarity with their weapons which made them seem like toys. The Vickers medium machine gun is an old and trusted weapon, virtually unchanged since the 1914–18 war. It can keep up continuous automatic fire almost indefinitely. The water-jacket surrounding the barrel prevents over-heating, and the heavy tripod makes a stable firing platform. During the field-firing exercises I had watched the machine gunners in action. Innocent-looking, the 'beaten zone' appeared, a long dust cloud hosing across the fields. Until you realised that there was not room in the dust cloud for a rabbit, let alone a man, to stay alive.

Mike Newall commanded the machine-gun platoon. Mike has dreamy eyes, which usually appear to be considering a problem somewhere in the middle distance, a slow smile and a steadfast refusal to be alarmed by anyone or anything. Visiting Generals or EOKA gunmen would draw from Mike the same courteous, efficient treatment. I knew he had distinguished himself in Cyprus by masquerading as a member of EOKA, to produce a great haul of forbidden arms and ammunition.

'Two taps right,' from Mike and the dust cloud had shifted fractionally across the landscape. They were fit too. I had seen them carry and trundle their heavy guns and tripods miles back to camp in the hottest part of the day. No one had lagged. A short time later they were all playing basket ball.

The anti-tank platoon had a chequered history. As an effective unit, that is capable of dealing with the sort of opposition we might well meet, it had only existed for a couple of months. Parachute troops were then very sensitive to tanks. Those who have read about the battle of Arnhem will understand why.

Without the determination and drive of Tubby Butler there would have been no anti-tank guns at all. The British Army possessed no proven weapon capable of knocking out the latest Russian tanks. It was generally known that Nasser had recently bought a number of these. When the original operation was first planned in August Tubby had foreseen that his brigade might well be opposed by Russian armour.

The Americans had invented the '106'. This is a recoilless 106 mm. anti-tank rifle which fires a heavy shell capable of penetrating 18 inches of armoured plate. A spotting shot is fired from a 0·5-inch machine gun mounted alongside the main barrel. As soon as the spotter is seen to strike the target the main charge is fired. It follows the exact trajectory of the spotter. If you have once seen the great glowing hornet buzz along its predestined path you never forget it. The target is doomed. The shattering black and orange clang of the explosion destroys it at once—infallibly.

The '106' was the answer. But in August the brigade had none. Tubby took part in some tough bargaining at the War Office. The '106' appeared and during the fortnight at home the battalion's anti-tank platoon became proficient with it.

Bill Hill, the lieutenant who commanded the anti-tank platoon had reason to be proud. In a short span of time his men had mastered their intricate, dangerous weapon. The danger from the '106' lay in the back blast when the main charge was fired. Any recoilless weapon must exert an equal explosive force in each direction. The back blast of the '106' had been enough to blow to matchwood a crate twenty yards behind it. But his platoon were cautious and efficient. Not for them the blood-and-thunder of the brigade field firing exercise. Their ammunition was too precious. Repeatedly they drove from camp thirty miles down to the southern range at Goshi. Each shot had been made to tell as the guns were aligned, spotting shots and main armament following identical paths.

Bill would return tired, dry and dusty from these outings. The platoon in their jeeps were obviously pleased with themselves. After all, not everyone knows that, given a chance, he can stop a fifty-ton Joseph Stalin tank dead in its tracks. Bill has a deadpan face and a penchant for throw-away lines. He ended a discussion in the mess on the merits of the Nicosia Club.

'Often think a well-placed EOKA bomb in that place would prune a lot of dead wood out of this Island.' And the poker-face crumpled hopelessly into the broadest grin, from the eyes to the corners of the mouth.

'Support' Company had not needed their major weapons against EOKA, but they had been committed early on to help maintain order.

From the start it was obvious that the Parachute Brigade approached things differently. 3 PARA were ordered to assist in police duties and curfew enforcement in the old city of Nicosia. Rioting and stone throwing had become frequent and troops had been issued with batons and shields to protect themselves while order was enforced. Support Company had none of it. When faced by a crowd of youths throwing stones they fixed bayonets. Lining the width of the street they marched slowly, inexorably towards the crowd which disappeared like morning mist.

The word must have gone around quickly, for surprisingly few attacks were made on units of the brigade during their time on the Island. The sad truth was that we suffered far more casualties in Cyprus as a result of accidents than from EOKA. Mistaken identity when fire was opened on operations, traffic accidents, and accidental discharge of weapons all took a remorseless toll.

The only obvious piece of 'bull' which met the eye as you wound along the dusty track into Tunisia Camp were two graves outside the guardroom. You later learned that they were dummies. A notice at their head carried the simple jingle:

> Ashes to ashes
> Dust to dust
> If EOKA don't get you
> 3 PARA must.

This was 3 PARA's assessment of the odds on survival, and was typical of the Toms' attitude to disaster generally. However you tried to minimise the chances, the accidents went on happening. You could only joke about it, or weep.

CHAPTER IV

GIN AND BITTER LEMONS

CYPRUS may have been a big mistake in every way, but as far as the battalion was concerned it had also been a huge diversion. Gone were the inevitable spring exercises on Salisbury Plain or Dartmoor. Gone the jumps onto Frensham or Figheldean Dropping Zones. The expected routine and tedium vanished. It was replaced by a different routine and tedium, but the Toms enjoyed change, and they had found it.

At first the contrast was not obvious. The wet, cold winter weather in Aldershot was exactly the same as that which they found in Cyprus. In a temporary camp site, nearer to the old city of Nicosia, flooding, mud and discomfort made them think back with relish to their barracks at home. Corunna Barracks in Aldershot had been condemned before the war as unfit for habitation by troops. None the less it provided a solid, if damp and insanitary overhead cover to the battalion. All the determination of the Colonel and second-in-command had secured only the most marginal improvements in the soldiers' lot there, and these only after repeated protests to the Garrison Engineers. Several years later, with the logic which typifies Treasury arrangements, thousands of pounds had to be spent on improvements, until the barracks was finally razed to the ground for rebuilding.

Corunna had its weaknesses, but cracked tarmac did cover the ground between the barrack blocks. And these were set high enough to prevent water actually coursing through them when it rained. In Cyprus the original camp could claim neither of these virtues. The tents leaked, water ran through the camp in rivulets, and a sea of mud engulfed everything. It was

54

with relief that the battalion eventually moved on to the escarpment near the airfield to establish Tunisia camp. 'A bit like an Arab cantonment' was how an officer in the Household Brigade described it, when his battalion took it over many months later. If whitewash had not proliferated, if some of the tents appeared to be grouped informally, and all of them were weatherbeaten, this was because their tenants were seldom at home to improve matters. The battalion spent most of its time out of camp. Training exercises, Internal Security operations and guard duties left little time for 'bull'. The Colonel preferred his soldiers to spend any spare time playing games or swimming in the Mediterranean rather than polishing up what was, at best, a few acres of Cyprus desert.

The camp, like the wise man's house, was founded on rock. A thin layer of reddish earth covered the underlying limestone, but not enough to hold the pegs. Pitching tents in such a situation was a considerable feat of engineering. Holes for each peg were drilled with compressors, and several thousand holes were required. But pitching tents was child's play compared with the problems of drainage. Enormous soakage pits were made to absorb the water from shower-baths and cookhouses, each of them quarried out of solid rock. Deep trench latrines are just what you would expect, and the depth should be about twelve feet. Only one Corporal on Bob Grainger's staff proved able to work a compressor in the reverberating depths of these chasms. His Augean task took many weeks and for much of it he was stone deaf from the shattering echoes of his machine.

Even before the change of camp occurred, the battalion was committed to the struggle against EOKA. No soldier ever enjoys assisting the Civil Power. The fact that soldiers are needed at all presupposes failure by the lawful means of government, and tension underlies the situation from the beginning. Cyprus was no exception.

Grivas had been clever. His studies of the mechanics of all good terrorist campaigns had convinced him that he must get the schoolchildren on his side. For in a very few years school-children become youths, and youths make good bomb-throwers and gunmen. During the first two years of his campaign he had concentrated on inciting schoolchildren to carry out quite simple orders in the cause of Enosis. A demonstration was needed, the children provided it. They distributed leaflets, acted as couriers, performed simple acts of organised disobedience to British rule. When 3 PARA arrived in Cyprus his campaigns of civil disobedience and carefully selected murders were both in full swing.

Horace McLelland, the Padre, had been one of the first of the victims of EOKA attacks within the ranks of the Brigade. He normally lived with 1 PARA in the adjoining camp. Horace knew how to talk to soldiers and was a welcome visitor everywhere. Whether he was taking a communion service in an olive grove, or talking to a platoon in the shadow of a dusty tent during one of his 'Padre's Hours', he held us all. His rounded Ulster vowels rang out in silence, for his sense of occasion was faultless. His text for Arnhem Sunday at the end of September was the end of the official account.

'. . . In attack most daring, in defence most cunning, in endurance most steadfast, they performed a feat of arms which will be remembered and recounted as long as the virtues of courage and resolution have power to move the hearts of men.'

Someone coughed, and it was as though a terrorist bomb had exploded in the silent congregation.

But to Horace this would hardly have been a new experience. Earlier in the summer he was involved in the funeral arrangements of the victims of the Paphos forest fire which had claimed many soldiers' lives. The funeral cortége wound slowly from the chapel at the Military Hospital round the outskirts of Nicosia, a journey of about three miles, to the military cemetery near the old established camp of Waynes Keep. Horace, dressed in his cassock, sat beside the driver reading his prayer book. Terrorism did not cross his mind for an instant as there were sadder, more immediate thoughts of the task ahead. They had become detached from the main cortége in Metaxas Square when suddenly the escort in the back shouted 'Bomb!'. The driver had the choice of putting his foot on the brake or the accelerator, and chose the brake. For what seemed like a minute they huddled up waiting for the explosion. Seconds later the bomb exploded in front of the Champ. Only Cypriots standing by were injured. The escort chased after two youths who ran away from the scene of the crime, but they escaped in the crowd. Horace looked to the injuries of the pitiful women and children at the roadside, and then took the funeral service as he had arranged.

Near the cemetery was the village of Ayios Dhometios, a notorious trouble spot. Any members of 1 and 3 PARA travelling between their camps and Nicosia were bound to traverse it. It looked such an open, innocent place. The long, straight road led you past the bungalow houses standing back in their own plots. All Cypriot houses have a large porch on the north side and here the family spends much of the long summer day, talking, drinking squash, wine or coffee, eating kebabs, talking and always talking. As you drove past they eyed you easily: they did not seem hostile, merely resigned. Then you passed the solemn church tower on the left, the honey stone warm and mellow in the midday sun. The school with its railings and noisy children, a few little dark shops and the coffee houses, and you were through the village climbing up onto the escarpment. The coffee houses always contained the same collection of white-shirted youths. Swarthy faces and black shiny hair accentuated the whiteness like a detergent advertisement, they sat there glowering, sneering. They were the new Grivas army.

It was in one of the little dark shops that it happened. A sergeant in the R.A.F. lived in the village with his family. Just before midday he went to the shop to buy some more paraffin. All domestic cooking is done on primus stoves and the Island's consumption of paraffin is huge. Regularly the sergeant had bought his fuel and he must have been carefully

57

watched. But the shop wasn't far away and his little boy, three years of age, went along with him for the walk.

About this time Captain Chiswell drove out of I PARA camp on the escarpment, heading for Nicosia, with an escort sitting in the back of the Champ. Peter Chiswell I knew well through David Hartley, his medical officer. Occasional meals which I had taken in the I PARA officers' Mess were always enlivened by the gusto and humour of his stories. Incidents seemed to dog Peter wherever he went, and David and he had become firm friends after one of the more dramatic of these. In a dawn search of a village on an Internal Security operation Peter led the way to the chief suspect's house. The front door was upstairs, approached by a steep wooden staircase and landing guarded with a wooden banister. Peter knocked and the door remained bolted. He took a flying kick at it and rebounded against the banisters, which parted in the miraculous fashion of banisters in Westerns and he fell to the ground below. He was severely concussed and broke a bone in his wrist. The arm was still in plaster.

The R.A.F. sergeant paid for his paraffin and headed for home hand in hand with his son. He was shot dead, in the back, as he left the shop.

Peter's Champ came past seconds later. They saw the little boy, frightened and astonished, crying beside his father's body. Over the way the coffee house crowd sniggered. It might well have been one of them. Peter and his escort ordered them all against the wall to be searched. Most obeyed, but one youth just shrugged insolently and remained seated. Peter watched his escort, with slung rifle, walk away, and thought he was going to ignore it. Suddenly the escort wheeled, unslinging his rifle as he did so. Crash! the butt slammed against the boy's jaw, shattering it. Then the search went on very quietly.

That was what EOKA did to you.

It was monotonous. The same sequence every time. A repeated, regular, careless journey was always to blame. The Medical Officer of the next unit down the road was killed as he drove back in his own car from visiting families in Nicosia. He made the same journey each Wednesday until, at a road junction on the edge of the town, he was shot in the back as he slowed down to turn the corner.

Careless journeys and careless weapon-handling cost us a lot of trouble.

'Bet he was choked,' was the response of one of the boys on hearing how a soldier had accidentally shot and killed his best friend. But this sort of thing could hardly be helped.

Whenever you went out of camp you carried a loaded weapon, and each vehicle carried an escort facing backwards. Weapons were loaded as soon as you left camp. Rifles and Bren guns were comparatively safe, as it was difficult to forget where they were pointing, and the triggers needed firm pressure to set them off. The nine-millimetre pistol and particularly the Sten gun were the culprits. Both were short and swung easily in any direction. The Sten gun could be set off by a good blow on the butt or by being dropped. The worst accidents had occurred when escorts had accidentally dropped or knocked Sten guns, sending a burst of fire through their drivers. Yet considering that the battalion had only handled live ammunition on the range before coming to Cyprus the number of accidents was not excessive.

It was an anxious time for those in charge, and the brunt of it was borne by the subalterns. Each was responsible for the weapon handling of the thirty-odd men in his platoon. The soldiers were aged between nineteen and twenty-five and many of them had not long learnt the elements of weapon training. The platoon commander personally checked his men's weapons on leaving and returning to camp. None of the subalterns would have admitted to anxiety had you questioned them, but it showed in unexpected moments. I used to look along the dining tables in our fly-blown Mess tent and study the faces at breakfast. Before the heat of the day descended, breakfast was the most sociable meal we consumed. Conversation ranged far away from our dusty surroundings, just like the conversations in Hall at Oxford, or the students' canteen at St. Thomas's Hospital. Yet something was different. The faces of the under-graduates and medical students had lacked the expression of alert boredom, of tired animation which the young officers' features so often wore in repose. Many of them were not long away from school, but they sometimes seemed a very old collection of young men.

As I gradually pieced together the story of what had gone before it was easy to see why.

Frustration was the keynote in the battle against EOKA. For the problem of Cyprus was a political one, and no amount of soldiers would ever solve it. It had been the battalion's duty to try to do so, or at least to prevent the terrorist campaign from breaking outside its unambitious, self-imposed bounds. Grivas did not set his sights very high. To begin with, he concentrated on murdering Greek Cypriots who were sus-pected of collaborating with the Security Forces. This and intimidation of the Cyprus Police Force were his first objectives. Neither was very difficult. Attacks on isolated village police stations, and a discreet shot or two in the back had very quickly spread the message among the friendly, humble, gregarious people of the Island. They were terrified of EOKA and would do nothing, nothing at all, to cross its path. Thus encouraged, Grivas had proceeded to carefully planned assassinations of British Forces personnel and, occasionally, of British civilians. He was careful to antagonise the Turkish minority in the Island as little as possible. The Turks disagreed passionately with the aim of Enosis, and would have fought to the last man to avoid it. Nevertheless even Grivas had his accidents, and these precipitated Greco-Turkish riots in which Cyprus was poised on the brink of civil war.

EOKA knew no rules of compassion or decency. Its murders were based solely on feasibility and it did not care who was the victim. Doctors, lawyers, peasants were all grist to the mill. The greater the outrage the better the effect. But the veterans in the brigade were contemptuous even of its ruthlessness.

'The Irgun would have run rings round this lot,' said an officer who had been through the Palestine debacle. There the Irgun organisation had increased the broad, horrible spectrum of terrorism by butchering the entire population of an Arab village and pushing the corpses down the village well. Such, or indeed any, heroics were far beyond the compass of EOKA. All its crimes were on a small scale and the cowardly manner of their performance was the only distinction they could claim. The sad truth is that nowadays if you tie a nationalist ticket round your neck and commit enough murders, however cowardly, to prove your point some philanthropist will bring your case to the United Nations and all your wishes will come true. The Irgun, Mau Mau and EOKA have proved this point repeatedly, a fact which their successors elsewhere have not overlooked.

Certain patterns of behaviour were bound to ask for trouble from EOKA. Any pre-arranged journey or repeated use of a particular place or route invited their attention.

Regular recreation was another favourite target for EOKA. A beach on the north coast, six miles to the east of Kyrenia, was wired off for bathing, and supposedly guarded. At weekends it would be thronged with troops bathing, sunning themselves or lying in the shade of three little 'bashas', reed-roofed shelters, in the middle of the beach. 3 PARA did not normally use the beach, as the Colonel regarded it with distaste and suspicion. But one Sunday, after climbing the peak of Buffavento, we had walked down there to meet the truck which was to drive us twenty miles back to camp.

The northern range was attractive to anyone interested in rock climbing. The hills were reminiscent in scale of the mountains in North Wales, a long spine of undulating peaks fringing the northern edge of the Island and trailing off along the 'Pan handle' to the east. The contrast with North Wales was underfoot. Instead of squelching over moss and rushes with their sodden suspended bogs, you approached the peaks through arid thickets of thorn and sparse pines. Grasshoppers rose in shoals from the stubborn, unyielding limestone soil. The rocks were clean and dry, often uncomfortably hot to the touch. Several ropes of climbers struggled up various routes on the south side of Buffavento, meeting up on the summit which was crowned by a ruined castle containing a most improbable well. Here a lonely forester kept watch for fires. His staple diet appeared to be a huge crock of salted olives, and rough bread.

We looked over to the north. Down the steep, pine-pricked slopes, the olive groves, open stubble fields, the coast road, and there in a little bay was 'Six-mile beach'. The startling blue of the sea looked most inviting. Half an hour later, sweat soaked and grubby from slithering down the dusty gullies, we reached the olive groves. As we did so we heard a muffled crack of an explosion towards the sea.

In some doubt we stumbled down the last mile to the beach. Chaos reigned. Angry, quiet groups of soldiers stood round the café and the collected trucks. A party had set off to hunt the olive groves. Another party had taken the casualty, a corporal in the R.A.F., to hospital in Nicosia. EOKA had contrived to mine the 'bashas' with mortar bombs and had skilfully concealed the detonating wire beneath the sand. When the bashas were seen to be full of troops the charges had been blown. Malcolm Elliott of the Field Ambulance had been dozing in the shade of one of them, the one in which, luckily, the charge failed to explode. Awoken by the roar of the bombs going off nearby, he found himself deserted. Everyone else had run for it. He tore off into the open and nothing further happened. The unfortunate corporal was lying over one of the bombs as it exploded and was mortally wounded. Malcolm supervised his dressings and went with him to hospital. Graham Owens, my old colleague of the 'P' course days, immediately took the Sappers' approach to the problem. Tracing back the wires, he unearthed the unexploded bomb which he disconnected. Wading far out, he dropped it in the sea, safe for ever. The other end of wire led right across the beach to the terrorists' 'hide', far up a bank near the road. They had probably escaped by car to the east. They were never caught.

The drive back through villages lined by giggling youths and children was the most humiliating part of it all.

It was not surprising that occasionally the troops saw red after these incidents. A Highland regiment tore a town apart after two of their number had been killed there. They used to drink from the communal tap after playing football each Saturday and EOKA could not resist it. They mined the tap so that when it was opened a bomb exploded underneath. The mayor, viewing his ruined shops and windows, protested to the commanding officer, but was stiffly told that the damage to his town was as nothing to that suffered by his regiment. This was the sort of harvest EOKA reaped in Cyprus.

It was a climbing party which was directly responsible for one of the worst attacks made on the Parachute Brigade. Paradoxically a climbing accident forestalled what might otherwise have been a disaster.

Our favourite peak in the northern range was Pentadactylos. The Greek word means Five Fingers, which is apt, for the mountain has five soaring buttresses of rock, each culminating in a summit. For several weekends in succession we had visited this lovely peak. The Welsh climbers said it reminded them of Tryfan, and the Scotsmen claimed it resembled the Cuillin in Skye. There was a profusion of possible routes and the rock was good. Many of the routes had been pioneered after the war by Colonel John Hunt, before he led the expedition to Everest. The approach to Pentadactylos was a drive of fifteen miles from camp and we started early.

The day began inauspiciously with the accidental discharge of a pistol as we left camp. Luckily the bullet thudded harmlessly into the ground and only pride was hurt. Early morning in Cyprus is the best time of the day. The air is cool as the salmon-belly pale dawn creeps over the sky. The hills stand cold and severe until the sun strikes them and shadows pick out the shoulders and gullies. All too suddenly it is hot and bright and long before midday you are looking forward to the sunset and colour again. It was still early when we turned off the main road to drive through the long, winding village of Kithraea, luscious with walnut trees and gardens. It is the only village on the Island to boast a perennial stream, but lovely as it looked, we knew it for a whited sepulchre, a stronghold of EOKA. The exhaust of the trucks re-echoed harshly from the buildings as we swished close to them through the twisting village street and startled faces peeped from the windows.

Some of the faces must have smiled in anticipation.

Five miles of twisting mountain track lay beyond the village. The surface became rough as it climbed tortuously to the top of the range and doubled back westwards towards the peak. We were able to bivouac within half a mile of the rocks. The pleasures of rock climbing are complex, but the 'Toms' enjoyed them all to the full. It was always a question of keeping the numbers down, as enthusiastic volunteers arrived in droves. We were lucky in having several experienced climbers in the Brigade to act as leaders, and it was shortage of climbing ropes which was the chief limitation. That first day was a carefree affair, each rope attacking a different route along the length of the cliff. I climbed with an officer from 1 PARA who shall be known as Jim. He led us securely up the right-hand pinnacle, steep dry pitches alternating with thorn and juniper ledges. The Toms approached it with élan. Just as you were about to belay you would find the man behind you had climbed half way up the pitch in question, ignoring the security of the rope completely. They were all fit and many of them natural gymnasts. Danger did not occur to them. There was no need to fall off, so what was there to worry about?

We lazed on the summit until the sinking sun hurried us down. David Hartley and his rope idled to such effect that they became benighted and the evening was raucous with shouts and studded with torchlight as a party climbed up to show them the easy way off the peak. To sleep out after our

64

enormous meal of 'compo' rations, with bright starlight, and the soft breath of wind sighing in the pines, was peaceful. It might have been any other climbing holiday, and EOKA seemed many miles away. Nevertheless we did post a guard throughout the long, quiet night.

Next day the ropes were re-arranged and a few of us were left spare, so we decided to cross a col and walk round the mountain on the north side to look for climbs on that side. We walked easily up through the Carob trees, through patches of stubble, and then scrambled up the rocks to the col. Down the other side was steeper for twenty feet and then we turned left to follow the cliffs to the west. David and I chatted of other climbs and wetter mountains. Jim who was with us spied a crack and began to climb it while we paused, watching him. The crack was in a corner, as if a great slab of the mountain was splitting off. For thirty feet it ran up, ending with a perched block, the size of a cabin trunk. Jim went rapidly up, 'laying back', his rubber soles confident against the flat, near vertical face. In a 'lay back' you hold one edge of the crack with both hands and walk up the face beyond it, pulling hard. It all depends on strong arms and friction. Provided the crack does not open unexpectedly it can feel strangely secure.

Up towards the block. He'd proved the point. It could be climbed, time to come gracefully down. No! He was going on, easily upwards, to the base of the perched block. The crack continued on its inner side.

'I don't think I'd touch that one.' Why was I tentative? Of course he mustn't touch the wretched thing. Bound to come away.

'Think it's okay.' A great muscular thrust as he said it, leaning back hard on the block.

I had been involved vicariously in one or two climbing accidents and this sequence of impending disaster was familiar. I had been there before. The masonry-noise of loosening rock, a gasp, and then the whole lot coming down. I was so pre-occupied with his fall, that great boulder coming on top of him, that I failed to notice it was going to hit me. My feet were knocked away like blades of grass. I was surprised to get up only grazed.

David and I ran over to the body. He couldn't possibly be alive. Blood welled from his nose and ear, and he turned blue. A long, glum silence. Then he groaned.

'Base of skull fractured and heaven knows what else,' said David.

'Nicosia's the only hope.'

Shouts produced a rescue party of adequate size. David's batman ran off to our bivouac to fetch a stretcher and was back in twenty minutes. But even with many experienced hands on the job it took an hour and a half to cross the col and return to the road. Everyone was covered in dust and sweat.

'I'll go with him, he's in my battalion,' said David.

'Very well. Pearson will drive.' We had the reserve 3 PARA stretcher Champ with us. The casualty on his stretcher was slid gently onto the racks at the back. David's batman climbed in as escort and Pearson took the wheel. Pearson came from Yorkshire and thought all climbers were barmy. But he was always ready to oblige, and, as Smith was engaged elsewhere, had come along to drive for me.

The Champ rolled slowly away down the bumpy track, and we returned to our bivouac. An hour later we heard an explosion down in the plain towards Kithraea. They must be well clear of the village by now. We never gave it another thought.

How wrong we were.

David was worried. Explaining the death of an officer in the battalion to his Colonel was not going to be easy. It seemed unlikely that the moribund figure in the back would survive even the short journey to Nicosia. His stertorous breathing was irregular and laboured. David made Pearson crawl the Champ over the agonising bumps in the track to lessen the shock for his patient. They took an hour to cover the five miles down to Kithraea, but at the beginning of the village the track improved and Pearson was able to accelerate.

'*SLAM*' as they rounded a corner. A blinding white flash and concussion. The windscreen shattered.

'——hell. ——EOKA up to their—tricks again,' gasped Pearson. His trousers were in ribbons and he had numerous grazes. Incredibly he was the only person hurt.

'Where's my pistol?' came a voice from the body at the back. Jim sat up, prepared to take on anyone.

'Round the corner and stop,' said David. They were afraid that machine-guns might open up from cover at the sides of the road. They stopped and nothing more happened. David and his batman ran back and saw how it had been. The bomb had been placed in a willow tree to one side of the road. The detonating wire led away behind a pig sty. The terrorists must have hidden there, waiting for the first truck to come down. Luckily they had misjudged their timing and the bomb had exploded too far behind the Champ.

Of course it was all our fault. Driving repeatedly up the same route through a village with an evil reputation such as Kithraea, we were asking for it. There was nothing David could do save drive on through grinning villagers, towards Nicosia. At least the explosion had bucked his patient up a little. He left him at the British Military Hospital, together with Pearson, who was feeling somewhat shaky by now. Bravely David then drove the Champ, with its shattered windscreen and torn canopy, back into the 3 PARA vehicle park.

Richard Dawnay greeted him as he arrived.

'What the hell d'you mean by bringing my stretcher Champ back in this mess?'

Poor David, two narrow shaves in as many hours had worn his sense of humour down to human proportions; as the Toms would say, he 'blew his top'.

We drove down later in the evening and passed uneventfully through the village. There was no sign of trouble and we did not suspect anything until we returned to camp and heard the full story from those who had witnessed David's return.

But for the accident to Jim, it was likely that a large truck would have led the way down. The EOKA men would have found it easier to time their explosion against a bigger target. The Champ was so low to the ground that they had probably been reduced to guesswork. The results of the bomb exploding above a 3-ton truck full of men were too horrible to contemplate.

The next week 1 PARA cordoned and searched Kithraea. The manner in which they did it left no room for doubt. They did not think the attempted assassination of their Medical Officer was funny. He had been travelling with his patient in a vehicle wearing conspicuous Red Cross markings. It was as well for the village that he had survived.

The battalion of the Household Brigade was becoming initiated into Internal Security operations at the time, and several of their subalterns went along with 1 PARA to study the form. From the subdued conversations which I later overheard, I gathered that if that was a cordon-and-search, give them a set-piece battle any day.

Several years later I found myself flying west out of Damascus. The Britannia climbed steadily after take-off and crossed the coast of Lebanon at a great altitude. A short time later tiny stars of light etched the outline of the 'pan-handle' on the sea below. The half-remembered village names unrolled and, suddenly, there was the long serpentine necklace of Kithraea beneath us. From that Olympian height, after only a few years, it was hard to recall the bitterness which those fairy lights had once symbolised.

Life on the Island was not all blood and thunder by any means. Much of it was routine, much boring. During the battalion's brief periods in camp we were thrown very much on our own resources for amusement. Incessant games of football and basketball, played by companies, platoons or sections, passed much of the time. 'Jimmy's' was a great solace afterwards.

A Cypriot contractor, who practised under the sobriquet 'Jimmy', was empowered to provide a café service and shop in a building in a corner of the camp. His negotiations were handled by the 'P.R.I.' Although the whole set-up, which involved the presence in camp of numerous Cypriots, constituted a big security risk, it was generally thought to be worth while. It certainly was for 'Jimmy'. He sold orangeade and 'Coke' by the gross, bacon and eggs, or steak and chips in scores in the evenings, and his shop had a large turnover in watches, cameras and all sorts of trinkets. It would have all been all right if his prices were just a little more reasonable. He held a monopoly of the market and could charge more or less what he liked. The Toms knew they were being robbed and would pay up uncomplainingly for months on end, until it proved too much to endure. Then the bright sparks would organise a robbery, always on the grand scale; nothing of any value would be left behind at all. Days of enquiry and search would follow these outrages. The Regimental Sergeant Major wore a long face and viewed everyone with suspicion until most of the loot was recovered. Among the hiding places which revealed it the Deep Trench Latrines were always prominent.

It was always said that whenever the battalion turned out on an Internal Security operation Jimmy passed the word in advance, through the Kykko telephone exchange, to any EOKA terrorists liable to be interested. No doubt, poor fellow, he did. Had he failed to do so he would probably have earned a bullet in the back for himself or his family. When the camp was sealed four days before we took off for Port Said Jimmy had been unceremoniously sacked. No doubt the facts had been passed on to anyone interested, as he went.

After a meal in 'Jimmy's' the Toms would often as not go on to attend the camp cinema. Our camp adjoined 1 PARA and the cinema was common to both battalions, so that an audience a thousand strong was a frequent occurrence. The screen was in the open and the audience sat on chairs or benches over a wide area. The projectionist wrestled with his apparatus in a little henhouse at the back. The films had been shown many times and usually came apart, so he had a good deal of wrestling to do.

David and I would go along after dinner sometimes, not so much for the entertainment of the film as that provided by the audience. The 'Toms' en masse and uninhibited were far more amusing than any film. An apt or obscene remark from someone at the back could be guaranteed to take the tension out of any moment of pathos or melodrama. Howls of execration always accompanied the breakdown of the projector. Anything smacking, however remotely, of sex was greeted with a masculine roar like a thousand rutting stags. The din which erupted at the showing of *Rock Around the Clock* must have been audible miles away.

The Nicosia Club and the *'Gourmet'* restaurant provided the equivalent of Jimmy's gastronomic delights for the officers of the battalion. The Nicosia Club felt dated. You expected a Somerset Maugham plot to be hatching beside the swimming pool or in the bar. The few British civilians on the Island could read the writing on the wall and a sense of apathy and resignation to the Emergency pervaded the place. It seemed to lead a charmed life from EOKA attacks. The bomb which Bill Hill had prophesied would 'prune a good deal of dead wood' out of the Island never materialized. The only dead wood removed thence eventually was Horace McClelland's old and trusted walking stick, which was stolen.

Several times David, Horace and I had dined there together. As the evening wore on we would walk out to dinner on the upstairs balcony. The night was still save for the stirring of crickets in the evergreens below. The bright stars of evening appeared overhead and the warm scent of Cyprus surrounded us. After a glass or two of Aphrodite it seemed idyllic. Until we remembered what was going on and why we were there. It was impossible to escape the feeling of melancholy which lay underneath every impression of that beautiful, tortured Island.

We paid off our taxi at the gate of Tunisia camp and I accompanied David along the rough track towards the gap in the wire separating us from I PARA.

'Listen,' he said. 'We've a marvellous bugler.'

And they had. Far off over the tents the single bugle began to play the 'Last Post'. The thread of sound rose from some lonely, sad well of silence, faultlessly into those soft familiar cadences. We stopped. There were so many memories evoked by that single call in the quiet night. The Cenotaph, Laurence Binyon, how many lives in how many wars? What teeming legions of Persian, Greek, Roman or Moorish armies had blown their bugles here? 'Then 'twas the Roman now 'tis I.' We said goodnight.

CHAPTER V

MALICIOUS MOCKERY

THE pursuit of EOKA by the security forces resembled a display of shadow-boxing. Most of the British hammer-blows landed on air, as their targets vanished into the forests, the farms, or the dark, twisting alleyways of the towns. For the essential element of surprise was usually denied them. Great cordon-and-search operations, involving thousands of troops and great movements of trucks, inevitably sent out vibrations which were picked up by the sensitive antennae of EOKA, and messages of warning could often be sent off ahead of the darkened convoys twisting through the night.

It was the extreme efficiency with which EOKA had permeated every organisation on the Island which made this possible. Postmen, telephone operators, contractors, foresters, policemen, all passed on what was required of them in the way of information. Each of them knew that it was literally as much as his life was worth to fail to do so. Nevertheless the big-scale operations had their successes. Early in 1956, Operation *Pepperpot*, based on Kambos in the western forests had accounted for several terrorists and a large quantity of arms.

The forests of Paphos and Troodos, in which the village of Kambos nestles, are a larger, denser barrier than the slender northern range. The steep, wooded slopes tower monotonously, wave on wave for about two hundred square miles. It is a bewildering country to the stranger. The secret valleys and nullahs wind indeterminately beneath a blanket of pine trees, and the slopes soar up evenly, at an angle of forty-five degrees to undulating crests between three and five thousand feet high. The few motorable roads and narrow one-way tracks are hidden in this sea of trees and you come across them with surprise. It was the perfect place for a mountain redoubt, and Grivas, the professional soldier, had not wasted his opportunity. The Monastery at Kykko in the centre of the area, acted as nerve-centre for EOKA. The old building gave the terrorists both physical and spiritual support. From its surroundings they could go forth to wreak vengeance on suspected informers. Thither they could return when pressure by the Security Forces became too hard on them in the towns of the plain. Surrounded by miles of forest, containing expertly camouflaged 'hides', and villages whose inhabitants were too terrified of EOKA to refuse the terrorists succour, their mountain redoubt seemed almost impregnable.

Early in the summer information came in of increased EOKA activity in the area. A fresh hammer-blow was prepared, under the code-name of *Lucky-Alphonse*.

'If ever an operation was misnamed,' said Mike Walsh, the commander of 'A' company, 'that was it.'

From the start of the operation tantalizing glimpses of success and crushing disasters stalked hand in hand. Leaving their camps at midnight, units of the Parachute and Commando Brigades drove into the area in darkness. Not a light was shown as the vehicles wound along the treacherous, narrow, winding mountain roads. By dawn some three thousand men were in position.

3 PARA were positioned on a ridge running southwards from Kykko. A road ran along it, beneath the crest. A few miles south the ridge curved away in a great crescent westwards, enclosing a bowl of forest two miles across, open at its northern end. To the east of the ridge the country fell away downhill, through the steep gullies covered with pine forest. The battalion was given the task of patrolling, searching and ambushing tracks in the area. Careful physical boundaries were assigned to each battalion and company, and ambushes set within these boundaries with orders to shoot on sight.

For forty-eight hours it followed the expected pattern. There were rumours of contact with EOKA, and suspicious noises were heard in the night. A platoon of 'B' company discovered a 'hide' and terrorist food stores. On the second evening, as the shadows stole up the slopes two separate shooting episodes occurred. The first was a single shot, in the north edge of the 3 PARA Sector, towards our boundary with 1 PARA. The second, a scattered volley.

The duty of searching the Monastery had fallen to 1 PARA. Horace McClelland, the Padre, accompanied the officer in charge of the search party, to soften the impact of the Army on the Ethnarchy. David Froud, commanding the patrol, was an imposing figure, with the proportions of a heavy-weight boxer —which he was—and over six feet tall. Ruggedly attired in smock and beret, and unshaven in the small hours, his appearance must have been terrifying as he hammered on the door. The servant who answered evidently thought so too. He scuttled quickly away down the dark passages to awaken the Abbot.

David turned to Horace.

'I think we're on to something here,' he said.

'Why?'

'That chap looked frightened.'

But the search was fruitless, despite the thorough scouring to which the Monastery and grounds were subjected. The old Abbot showed Horace round the chapel, pointing out with pride his various relics and treasures. Later on he added to this kindness by filing an official complaint that a jewelled knife of great value had disappeared during the search. He mentioned that the Padre accompanying the Security Forces had shown great interest in the history of the Monastery in general, and in this knife in particular. Horace thought he had probably lost nothing at all, and was simply piling on the agony for the unrewarding search of his premises. Doubtless he had sighed with relief when the searchers left. The searchers had been confident of finding hidden arms or terrorists.

Perhaps it was this frustrating start to the operation which spurred on the Sergeant Major from 1 PARA. He may have had other reasons or suspicions prompting him to act as he did. Late in the afternoon of the second day he drove in his Champ south down the road, out of his Battalion Area, and then led a patrol, consisting of a few members of his company Headquarters, up a gully beside the road.

The 3 PARA ambush was well sited to cover the track up the gully, and the young soldier on guard was alert. When he saw movement, which could only be EOKA as other movement was forbidden, he fired once.

The Sergeant Major fell dead, and the man behind him was seriously wounded.

That was the single shot.

At about the same time a patrol of 'C' Company was returning to its base, down on the east side of the ridge. They had no wireless, for the scale of issue of walkie-talkie sets was not generous at that time. Across a deep ravine, three hundred yards away they saw a group of figures moving off, away from them. They opened fire without scoring a hit, and set off in pursuit, downhill, then up again to where the terrorists had been seen.

Equipment lay scattered around. Binoculars, a smart Sam Browne belt, a revolver and numerous papers and notebooks. Obviously this was an important find, but how to convey the news? A man was sent at the double up the hillside, towards the road at the top of the ridge. It was not until his report reached the Colonel that the scattered volley was explained. The wireless network became hectic as a cordon was organised to block the escape of the fugitives. Probably it was too late, and they had already crossed westwards into the open bowl of forest, even as the news of the encounter was being relayed within the battalion.

The abandoned equipment acted as a spur to furious activity. Two days later the report came back from Nicosia that the notebooks were in fact the diaries of Grivas himself. In his latest entry Grivas complained of trouble with his arthritis, and revealed the desperate pressure to which the search had subjected him. Only the previous night he had apparently all but stumbled into a 'C' Company ambush. Efforts to track him down were redoubled.

At the same time tragedy struck again. A 1 PARA truck drove off the narrow track and tumbled end-over-end down the precipitous hillside for about five hundred feet. Three of its occupants were killed. Bob Grainger's Ration Truck followed a similar fate. His staff were scattered like chaff among the pine trees, but all survived. The rations were never seen again.

Worse was to follow. The news that Grivas was somewhere in the cordon had led to large reinforcements being drafted to the area. The Norfolks, Gordons, Royal Engineer units and a detachment of the R.A.F. Regiment joined the search. Many of these men were new to the routine of cordon-and-search and formed an outer cordon to the south of the great bowl of forest which was being quartered, up and down every exhausting gully, by 3 PARA.

'D'you remember, Mike, we searched every blooming yard of that place?' Years afterwards the exasperation, frustration and fatigue of it lived again in the Colonel's voice as he recalled it. Outside Mike Walsh's drawing room at Camberley the conifers dripped sullenly in the autumn drizzle. The Colonel, now a Brigadier, put down his coffee cup, and for an instant a far-away look crept into the eyes of both men. They were transported two thousand miles away and six years back in time, to those useless, tantalizing hours of hunting around beneath the hotter, angrier pines.

The hunt went on for several days, and Press reporters and photographers joined the searchers, to provide cover. The incipient capture of Grivas was big news. In the early dawn a photographer and reporter from the *Daily Telegraph* accompanied one of the 3 PARA Company Commanders as he visited his outposts. Suddenly the reporter pointed out a figure crawling off through the forest, wrapped in a blanket. None of our troops were in the area and it must be a terrorist. The

Company Commander fired one shot with his Sten gun, a notoriously inaccurate weapon. The crawling figure dropped dead. They ran up and were appalled to find the flashes of the Norfolk regiment on the body beneath the blanket. It transpired that the Norfolk soldier, delirious with fever, had left his position and was walking aimlessly around in the forest. During a cordon-and-search you could not afford to walk aimlessly, anywhere.

Various false alarms followed. Eventually it seemed that the terrorists might have escaped southwards towards the positions of 40 Commando, and their 3-inch mortars pounded the area where Grivas and his party might be hiding. It seems likely that the explosions of these mortar bombs in that tinder-dry country set fire to the forest. Grivas later claimed to have lit the fire himself, but this idea matured for a suggestively long time in his cunning mind before he published it abroad. Whatever the cause, the fire rapidly increased its hold, despite all efforts to contain it. The professional Cypriot Foresters were called in to help, for the technique of fighting fire in the resinous, dry trees is a specialised business.

Next morning Mike Walsh and his second-in-command were driving, above the fire, along a one-way mountain track which led horizontally westwards beneath the crescent-shaped ridge. They were to attend the court of enquiry on the dead Norfolk soldier. Smoke wreathed the track as the firefighters beat at the flames from either side. A scout car blocked the track and all the vehicles came to a halt.

Suddenly it was a shambles. The fire crossed a gully beneath them and leapt up hill at forty miles an hour, accelerating all the while with its own draught. A dozen men perished in as many seconds, and the figures scattered from the vehicles on the track. Mike ran down, through the fire, to escape with severe burns. His second-in-command and driver ran uphill and were engulfed by smoke and flames, and both died.

The news spread faster than the flames. The Colonel made for the scene by a circuitous detour, avoiding the blocked track. Basil, my predecessor as Medical Officer, was lowered into the carnage from a helicopter and did great work treating the numerous casualties who still lived. The Colonel and a Company Commander from the Gordons, whose men had suffered severe losses, organised the clearing of the track so that the injured could be evacuated to hospital. Trucks were ruthlessly pushed over the edge to go crashing down the smoking hillside. Horace was about to take a Communion service at 1 PARA Headquarters when the news came through. He cancelled his service and drove off southwards. As soon as he arrived, a glance at the Colonel told him that the battalion had suffered. Horace willingly took on the awful task of telling the widow of the dead officer that her husband had died. She had only arrived in Cyprus to join him a week previously.

Perhaps the thought of what he had to do affected his driving, for as they swung round one hair-pin bend after another the soldier travelling as escort asked:

'Excuse me, Padre, but have you ever driven a Land-Rover before?'

And that, really, was the end of *Lucky-Alphonse*. As previously described Horace was attacked by EOKA during the funeral cortége, and then at the sad graveside service nineteen coffins were lowered into a common grave. The score was not even then complete, for most of the severely burned patients in hospital in Nicosia subsequently died. All in all the operation had cost about thirty lives and EOKA, as far as could be seen, had escaped Scot free. For another week the search for Grivas and his confederates went on, but nothing came of it. They had vanished. Even if they had been destroyed by *Lucky-Alphonse* history might well have been no different. Grivas had done his work well. The Hydra he had created had many heads, and grew strong on the emotion of Enosis. Severing a few of the heads would not have ended the tide of murder and violence which he had unleashed with such efficiency. Perhaps that tide would never rest. Seven years later the full flood came in when internecine Civil War flared between Greeks and Turks over Christmastide in 1963. There were several hundred casualties and, as a final irony, the Parachute Brigade, among others, came back to the Island to restore order.

But in 1956 it seemed simpler. The hard core of terrorists were few in number. *Lucky-Alphonse* might not have accounted for any, but it had disrupted the gangs in Troodos and rendered them incapable of coherent effort for some time. To the soldiers the defeating thing was the thoroughness of the EOKA ground-work, the absolute indoctrination of the youth of Cyprus.

For this the British administration must bear the blame. Greek had been left to teach Greek, and nobody knew what they were saying as they did so. Skilled interpreters were so few on the Island that interrogation of EOKA suspects early in the emergency presented a severe problem. Ignorant of what was going on under their noses, the British had not raised a finger to correct or oppose the subversion of the children, and when we realised what had happened it was too late. This failure to learn the language of a colonial people was an elementary error. At one time the presence of a Greek 'E' in your handwriting was said to be worth a place in the Foreign Office. It would have been as well, for Cyprus at least, if the Colonial Office had used the same criterion for their candidates.

Against EOKA, cloak-and-dagger methods sometimes brought the greatest rewards. Setting a thief to catch one was usually worth while. Mike Newall of Support Company was involved in the earliest success of this kind. He teamed up with an EOKA turncoat, and set off to meet the leader of a village gang. After much driving around in darkness in an assortment of cars, and eventually a bus, the gang were persuaded to hand over their supply of arms. This was allegedly to reinforce the gangs in Nicosia at the express orders of 'the old man' —Grivas. With his dark hair, dreamy eyes and slow smile Mike would have made a convincing terrorist. His colleague, the ex-EOKA man, was achieving three ambitions by his treachery. His long police record was erased, he made a lot of money by giving valuable information to the Security Forces, and he indulged to the full his native passion for intrigue.

Eventually the dénoument arrived. The arms were safely loaded into the bus and Mike, brandishing an automatic pistol, strode out in front.

'*Stamata!*' his only word of Greek. 'Halt!'

The pistol gleamed ominously in the headlights. After a pregnant pause they all came quietly. Fourteen weapons, and their owners, were not going to shoot anyone in the back for some time to come.

It was a Support Company ambush which achieved one of the early successes on a major operation. Sergeant Howse of the machine-gun platoon was responsible. A quietly-spoken man with a mild manner and phlegmatic disposition, he did not strike you immediately as a tough professional soldier. But when you had watched him exerting his quiet authority on his machine-gunners in action, or racing lightly and nimbly round the basket-ball pitch, you revised this hasty judgement. Here was a man of parts.

The ambush was laid, at night, on one of the winding forest tracks near Kykko. Terrorists might well use the track and the sergeant had lookout men posted on either side who could communicate with him by tugging a length of string. In absolute silence they waited. The slow hours passed. Each little sound, the usual sounds of a forest at night, assumed huge importance as the painful time dragged by.

A tweak on the string. Footsteps! A man carrying a heavy weight. As the man came opposite him the sergeant moved silently out from behind cover and clapped his pistol to the man's head.

'Drop that.'

A gasp of astonishment and he dropped it. A Bren gun. And he was festooned with bombs and ammunition.

All this, recent and painful as much of it was, lay in the past when I arrived back in Cyprus from Abingdon in September. I assimilated the facts, but none of the feeling of Internal

Security Operations. Operation *Sparrowhawk* quickly corrected my ignorance.

Sparrowhawk began, with deliberate subtlety, exactly as the Brigade Field Firing exercises had done a week before. A large part of the Parachute Brigade drove to the east coast beyond Lefkoniko, and after most of the soldiers had bathed in the sea, all bivouacked for the night.

In the Battalion Headquarters Airborne Shelter the Colonel held an 'O' Group. The Tilley lamp threw its hard, uncertain light on the cluster of brown faces, faded maroon berets with their gleaming pointed badges, and dusty smocks. Outside in the darkness the battalion made ready for the night. Sleeping bags were unrolled, each Company Colour Sergeant issued food to his hundred-odd soldiers, vehicles were parked in groups, while around the perimeter prowled the sentries with loaded rifles and fixed bayonets. Odd flashes of torchlight lit up the gloom. Any Cypriot listening in the darkness beyond might have heard the revving of engines, an occasional oath, a burst of laughter, or shouted instructions to the drivers. With luck he would think that we were to spend another day harmlessly shooting at oil drums on the inland plain.

In the Airborne shelter the Colonel unfolded his plan. The Intelligence Section had produced a series of marked maps, and these were passed round. The dispositions were clear. The battalion was to cordon-and-search the area around Kalogrea, a village lying on the northern, seaward, side of the northern range. We were to move into position before dawn next day and 'dominate the area'. I looked round the friendly, alert, familiar faces. It seemed incongruous. In a few hours these men would surround those innocent-looking black dots which marked the village on the map. Anyone trying to escape would probably be shot dead. In this easy, cheerful gathering the orders had been given. Now the consequences were inevitable.

In darkness, and a dense fog, the battalion drove over a pass in the northern range, turned westwards, and had cordoned the village by the time dawn crept into the sky next morning. In the half-light Dick Stevens, commanding 'B' Company, strode up the village street at the head of a patrol. From a dark alley to one side came the crack of an explosion, and a small-calibre bullet whizzed past his head. The patrol dashed off in search of the would-be murderer, but found no one. Perhaps it was a half-hearted attempt on the part of a schoolboy to win glory. Nevertheless Dick's sense of humour is on the wry side at the best of times, and this was not a tactful welcome. His company was to be responsible for searching the village during the days ahead. If the search was carried out with more than usual thoroughness, that would be no more than the village deserved.

Battalion Headquarters was situated down near the beach. The medical Airborne Shelter was assembled and the Champ parked alongside. Not for long, for as the trucks were backing off the road a soldier was crushed between a stone wall and one of the mudguards. Smith drove off to Nicosia with the injured man. Our troubles had begun.

After that it fell quiet for a few hours, until in mid-morning we were visited by His Excellency. As Governor of Cyprus Field Marshal Harding had won the affection and admiration of all soldiers on the Island, both by his personal courage, and even more by his forthright handling of the Emergency, and the interest and encouragement he gave to the troops involved. If the Cyprus problem had degenerated into a soldier's affair it was as well to have a soldier in charge. And what a soldier! His helicopter swung low over the hills and landed in a flurry of dust alongside the beach. The down-draught from its rotors shattered some improvised 'bashas' on the shingle into so much flotsam. Beneath these some of the Sappers, ingenious as always, had been sheltering from the hot morning sunlight. The rotors stopped swirling and out stepped a short, compact figure with an unmistakable scarlet band round his cap. The Colonel, Adjutant and Company Commander walked forward to greet him. However, his first action was to walk over to the pulverized 'bashas' and apologise to the Sappers for their destruction.

He shook hands with the Colonel, and the other officers were re-introduced. He had met them all before on other operations. Then he moved on to inspect Battalion Headquarters. Each department was covered carefully, a few searching questions and he passed on. Our turn arrived. A firm handshake and penetrating glance from the kindly grey eyes.

'What can you manage to cope with here?' His glance roved over our few pieces of equipment. He must have inspected thousands of Regimental Aid Posts, but gave the impression that this, to him, was a novel and interesting experience.

'Well, sir, we can't provide much more than glorified first aid, on our own. That and minor sick are about all our equipment will cover. We hope to evacuate anything more serious to the Field Ambulance.'

'I see. What happens on an Airborne Operation?'

'Then a section of the Field Ambulance and Field Surgical Team may come with us.'

So it went on. Like a 'viva' in Finals all over again. But no medical examiners had been as alive, as interested as this. When the helicopter disappeared over the slopes to the west we were all left strangely heartened.

In the afternoon I went up to the village where the search was well under way. On the school play-ground a Danert wire enclosure had been erected, to contain suspects awaiting interrogation. The Drum Major was supervising the finishing touches as the last angle-irons were driven home. It looked efficient, business-like, sinister. Two thousand years ago the Roman Centurions were efficient too.

'B' Company was searching the village. In their keenness to find the pistol which had fired the shot at their Company Commander they were leaving nothing to chance. Below the school was a row of little houses, their backyards open to the sky. From my eyrie on the playground I could see it all. A few hens scratched around disconsolately in the heat of the day. One of the Toms was methodically going over the nearest backyard. With his bayonet he prodded through a pile of rubbish. Vegetable stalks, tins, and old rags lay in chaos around him.

The old owner of the house turned her wrath on him. She was a desiccated, shrivelled old woman: women age quickly in the Mediterranean. Life had been hard and this was the end. Her few possessions were in peril.

'*Tipote! Tipote!*' she squawked from the doorway. 'Nothing! Nothing!'

The Tom prodded calmly on, regardless.

'*Tipote! Tipote!*'

'Aw shut up, you old bag! I can't see any bleeding teapots.' And, in disgust, he went on to repeat the performance in the yard next door.

Similar scenes were being enacted on every side. Cupboards, lofts, rafters, fireplaces, all were ransacked. Pathos greeted me at every turn as I walked up the street with Holden, my faithful batman, with his loaded rifle at my side. Sullen faces glowered at us from the dark doorways and it was humiliating, if salutary, to feel so hated. Then a sergeant came up to us from a side alley.

'There's a kid in here I think you'd better look at, sir.'

We followed into a surprisingly large living room and in one corner, on the stone floor, covered in flies, lay a pale, emaciated child of about eighteen months. The women sat around, venom in their eyes. I felt the feeble little pulse.

'*Iatros. Iatros.*' A rustle of noise went hissing from mouth to pursed mouth. And suddenly it was all different. A doctor at large in the village was a rarity, and in a matter of minutes I was plunged into a hectic round of visits. The village teemed with disease, both real and imaginary, and sorting this out, with the aid of Sergeant Rabet's phrase book, very soon became a full time job.

My loyalties were divided. The battalion with its scattered

companies was my first commitment, but the medical plight of the villagers was more pressing. They were such real, unaffected and sincere people. Like country people everywhere their inherent good manners kept showing through the film of dislike and distrust between us, but their menfolk were being rounded up for questioning and hatred was never very far beneath the surface.

The questioning was to be carried out by various interpreters, on the advice of two embittered Greek Cypriots from a neighbouring village. These men had lost several relatives at the hands of EOKA, and were bent on evening the score. They stood up in front of the suspects squatting in the pen of Danert wire on the school playground. There was a pause, and then the larger and more saturnine of the brothers broke into a harangue. For several minutes he held forth on the evils of EOKA. Then, after the manner of a Welsh Hwyl run riot, he began to pick out miscreants left and right. Clearly a lot of scores were being settled, regardless of EOKA or anything else.

'Stop!' The Colonel had been standing by watching with mounting wrath as the farce unfolded. 'I won't have this charade. We'll do this thing properly or not at all.'

The two men were summarily dismissed and the interrogation proceeded on more orthodox lines. It was abortive and no disguised EOKA men were discovered.

So the search went on.

The village priest, himself ex officio a leading suspect, was one of my first casualties. He was the chief beekeeper, and his hives were an obvious hiding place for arms. When they were searched he was severely stung. He peeled off layer after layer of black, malodorous garments, and finally a pair of grey pinstripe flannel trousers, to reveal the damage. Later in the day we joined forces as he administered the last rites to an old lady dying of uraemia. Even his buildings could not be respected. From the summit collaboration of Makarios and Grivas, down to the humblest village priest and the village EOKA gang, the terrorists and the church were hopelessly intertwined. The local priest automatically headed the list of suspects and his church was among the likeliest hiding places.

When Smith drove the stretcher Champ down to Anti-phonitis monastery, above the village, I thought this must be an exception. Dark cypress trees and gnarled olives framed the buildings in a warm, fertile hollow in the hills. On the horizon the Taurus mountains in Turkey loomed darkly, separated from us by the impossible, bright blue of the Mediterranean. The gentle dome of russet tiles on the strong honey-coloured walls, solid shadows and dark windows, seemed to grow out of that happy ground. Nothing mean or sordid, like terrorism, could happen here.

But the platoon whose duty it was to search the place had levered up most of the old flagstones just to make sure.

Disappointment and disaster intruded again before long. One of our men searching the hillside near the old monastery fell down a fifty-foot cliff and had to be carried, concussed and bleeding, down to the village. That night worse followed. In another tragic mistake about boundaries a patrol walked into an ambush set by 1 PARA in a gully to the west. One man who walked into the fire of a Bren gun at close range survived for less than an hour.

It was 2 PARA who scored the major success of *Sparrowhawk*. Their task was to search the country near Kyrenia, between that pleasant seaside town with its water-lapped castle walls, and the mountains of the Northern Range. At the foot of the mountains lies Bellapais, a village rich in walnut and olive trees surrounding another ancient monastery. Somewhere in this delectable stretch of country it was known that an EOKA gang had gone to ground. Only a week or two previously in a brutal ambush on the road to Kyrenia they had killed two British civilians, one of them a woman.

Searching a lonely farmhouse, the soldiers of 2 PARA noticed a difference between the outside and inner dimensions of the walls. A hole was quickly knocked in the false inner partition and one of the 'Toms' peered into the darkness. A frightened pair of Greek Cypriot eyes stared back.

'Cor, who's got a grenade? Got a grenade, wack?'

Fortunately for the EOKA men hiding inside no one could produce a hand grenade. They all surrendered. The farm was demolished, to the accompaniment of tears and wailing by the women and children who also lived there. Malcolm Elliott of the Field Ambulance was acting as Medical Officer with the 2 PARA company and witnessed it all. He was overwhelmed by the futility of the thing, the homeless weeping children, the dynamited building, and the ever widening ripples of misery. The EOKA gang was a mere symptom of the disease which racked Cyprus. Snuffing it out was no more likely to effect a cure than sneezing into a handkerchief to cure a cold.

For a further week *Sparrowhawk* continued in the country west of Kyrenia. We searched several villages in vain, and it seemed to be degenerating into a pleasant, but ineffective waste of time. Luckily medicine was always in demand. '*Iatros! Iatros!*' And off we went again, eking out our dwindling supplies of '*Hapia*' (pills) with the odd '*Inesin*' (injection), in which the villagers had a complete and childish trust. Medical problems hit the aether one morning, when a demand from '*Starlight*' of the gunners for '*Starlight* assistance' came over the wireless network: this turned out to be Basil, involved with a confinement in an isolated village. No Gunner, or any other Regiment, carries midwifery equipment among its Medical Kit, so we retrieved a few oddments from the Field Ambulance which was camped nearby, and Smith drove towards the village at top speed. Of course we arrived too late, but I would not have missed that scene for anything.

Basil, with his huge frame and shock of fair hair, was acting as ringmaster. His circus was taking place in a low, dark one-roomed house, illuminated by one oil lamp and the light which diffused through the doorway. A huge sow snuffled outside the door. Apparently she had just been put out for the occasion. In the gloom within the delivery was just complete. Three small children stared in fascination over the end of a low bed where the exhausted mother lay holding her baby. Various old aunts and grannies pottered about, dispensing preserved fruits and glasses of cold water. This was a universal token of gratitude or celebration in Cyprus. A huge, rather sickly fruit, or walnut preserved in syrup, handed on a three-pronged fork, together with a large glass of exquisitely cold water.

'*Efharisto! Efharisto!*'—the same word as Eucharist, meaning 'Thanks'. The baby, a lively dark-haired boy, was to be named Vasilios after Basil. The broad face beneath the shock of hair beamed back at them. Everybody smiled.

On occasions such as this Holden's loaded rifle seemed rather an insult.

I have attended one Cypriot confinement since then. That, too, had its lighter side. It was while I was a house surgeon in Worcester after I was demobbed. The patient once again was delivered of a splendid boy, and her name was Grivas! She was a distant niece of the 'Old Man'. Somewhat ruefully I explained, before she went home, that I had spent some time hoping to meet her uncle. Without success.

In the hot Cyprus dusk it was difficult to force 'Compo' rations down. So occasionally Gerald Mullins, the Adjutant, and I would make curry for Battalion Headquarters. The tins of stew, meat and vegetables, and steak and kidney pie which formed the bulk of 'Compo' were emptied out into a huge bowl, boiled up, and rendered slightly more palatable with various additions. One night there by the beach I rashly added a tin of anchovies.

'Perhaps not another time, Doc,' said the Colonel. 'But anything's worth a try.'

As he said it a machine-gun stitched the night somewhere to the west of us. He frowned.

'Get on to them, Gerald, and find out what's going on.'

It transpired that Cypriots were breaking the curfew imposed by a unit in the neighbouring village. Bursts of Bren gun fire down the main street were encouraging them to keep indoors.

'Present my compliments and tell them I think it's childish and dangerous. Will they please stop.'

They stopped, and the silence was broken only by the gently lapping waves and tireless crickets buzzing in the trees.

And so, a few days later, the tragi-comedy of *Sparrowhawk* petered out. The Parachute Brigade drove back over the Northern Range to its dusty camps in the plain around Nicosia. Peace returned to those fertile groves along the north coast, broken only by sundry EOKA murders of Cypriots who were thought to have afforded us the slightest help.

Murder and sudden death ceased to interest the battalion for a few days after Operation *Sparrowhawk* ended. In the dusty confines of Tunisia Camp, near the airfield outside Nicosia, the soldiers made ready for whatever might happen next. Their weapons were cleaned and handed in to the company arms stores. These were small, scattered Nissen huts, one to each company, where a hundred men's arms were checked, stored and constantly guarded. If weapons and ammunition were the most vital of their stores, they were by no means the only ones in need of overhaul. Clothes were laundered, boots repaired and deficiencies in personal kit made good by Company Colour Sergeants. Depending on the reason for the deficiency the man in question either did or did not pay for the replacement.

It was during this interlude that I first really noticed the Toms' civilian clothes. Each man had accumulated, somehow, more or less complete civilian attire. This was no mean feat, as none of it had come with them on that original flight from Aldershot, back in February. There had not been room for luxuries like odd clothes. With the unerring taste of all young men they had selected a striking cross-section of avant-garde garments, steering a delicate passage between humdrum and outrageous. Startling check shirts, drain pipe trousers and suede shoes were in profusion. And it was always the same. When we eventually returned home to Aldershot I used to watch in amazement on a Friday evening as the boys went off to catch the London train. Haircuts of surprising length would emerge from beneath their berets, and fur collars and winkle pickers replaced battle dress. In a matter of minutes the whole battalion of Toms were transformed into as many Teds. The process was reversed on Sunday night, and on Monday the strictly military turn-out of everyone made you doubt whether the weekend had ever been.

The interval was not long. A week after our return from the north coast we were briefed for Operation *Foxhunter*. This was to be a fresh onslaught on the familiar stamping ground in the Troodos forests. By now I had seen enough to know what was coming.

After darkness had fallen a long convoy of trucks wound westwards from the camp. For twenty-five miles they made fairly quick progress using sidelights only. The last fifteen miles of winding mountain road were covered in complete blackout. Luckily there was a thin moon shining, which made progress a little quicker. The front seat of the Champ was warm, and sleep dragged again and again at my eyelids as the slow miles passed. Only the knowledge that if I dropped off the driver would immediately follow suit kept me awake. In the early hours of the morning on 25th October we arrived in Kambos. The cordon settled like a wraith around the village and waited. Tension rose as the sky lightened over the ridge to the east. Now was the time for any EOKA men, finding themselves surrounded, to make a bolt for their hides in the forest. Uneventfully night became day.

> Thy dawn, Oh master of the world, Thy dawn
> The hour the lilies open on Thy lawn.

To one person at least it was eventful. My memory is like an untidy attic full of vivid impressionist canvases, piled higgledy-piggledy, unframed, but dated and signed with place-names. 'Early morning in Kambos' is near the top of the heap. The startling whitewash of the school, dun tiles, yellow walnut leaves and fading green of the vines slants upwards to the dull rust of autumn trees on the skyline high above; silhouetted against the pale cool blue of the morning sky. As I came out of the police station which housed Battalion Headquarters this was what I saw. But lovely or not, Kambos had an EOKA record as long and bad as any village on the Island. It must be searched.

And it was. The same unhappy scenes that I had witnessed on Operation *Sparrowhawk* were repeated. The village had been subjected to two previous searches and the inhabitants reacted more bitterly than the northern peasants had done. In the pleasant, narrow, winding street, its balconied houses and over-hanging eaves reminiscent of villages in the Alps, the atmosphere was charged. From the coffee house and shop on the corner smouldering glances were directed at us as the job of hunting went on. The hunting itself was fruitless, and interest moved to the neighbouring hamlets in the deep, pine-filled valley.

Medicine was still in demand and our practice in the village snowballed with each succeeding day. The village school-master became my chief interpreter, and despite the sergeant's phrase-book was a very necessary part of the show. Patients' replies to my few stock questions such as 'Where is the pain?' or 'Have you got diarrhoea?' were always reeled off at top speed, and ran to several paragraphs. I would lamely rejoin ' *Then enkatalaves*'—'I don't understand', and send someone off to find him. In an uneasy way we became friends. I treated his child for tonsillitis, and his wife presented me with a huge cake. When the patients had at last come to an end, we would talk on about this and that, but when I tried to lead conver-sation round to politics, EOKA and the village a strange veil descended. He would look into the distance, smile slowly and talk about something entirely different.

I wondered how many pistols were trained on his back.

For the companies supplying the cordon the old routine unrolled again. Search by day. Ambush by night. Most of them had been to this very area before and knew these toe-stubbing slopes intimately. But the soldiers were not bored. When you are carrying a loaded weapon eight hours a day, up and down three thousand feet of hillside, sometimes in silence, sometimes in tense anticipation, boredom is not one of the many emotions to which you are exposed. Heat, dust, water shortage and sore feet may make you exhausted, fed up or bloody-minded, but the contrast between fundamental pains and pleasures is enough to keep boredom away. To drink water, even the tepid, aluminium-tainted stuff in the water-bottle at your waist, can be the ultimate in delight if you first become severely dehydrated.

For three days it went on. Noises and movement were reported in the night. One or two suspicious tracks and a 'hide' were found. On the third evening the Colonel was to hold a conference in the village police-station, and all the Company Commanders would come in from their positions in the hills around. We thought it an auspicious occasion for a curry. A re-supply of curry-powder was organised from Nicosia, and the stores were assembled beneath a tarpaulin outside. I went into the village shop to purchase wine.

'Yes, sir! We have ver' good white wine.' Overwhelming politeness from a satanic-looking character behind the counter.

I eyed the pale brown liquid dubiously. It looked like sherry. I took a couple of bottles.

'Have you anything else?'

'Oh yes, sir. We have black!' And I departed with several bottles of the umber fluid.

It would all have been fine if we had used our old familiar curry powder. The tins from Nicosia were of treble-strength and the resulting curry correspondingly fierce. The officers crowded into our dining-room were drenched with sweat before the dish was finished, and both white and black wine were drained in the battle against the flames within. The conference went with unwonted ease, and literally breathing fire and brim-stone the participants returned to their bivouacs.

Next morning the rumours began. We were going back to camp to prepare for an airborne operation. We were to stay in Kambos for a further fortnight. We were to return to England next week. Gradually the plot clarified and the likely moves became obvious. Israel had invaded Egypt and the Ultimatum had been issued.

At midday on the 29th of October we were ordered to pack up ready to return to Nicosia. That evening, after the drive back in the clear afternoon sunlight, speculation and rumour permeated every Mess and department of the battalion.

Chapter VI

GUNPOWDER, TREASON AND PLOT

THERE is only one nation in the world to whom Middle East politics are transparently clear: Israel. The entire political and military effort of this small nation is directed to one end: survival. On 29th October, 1956, for her own ends, Israel launched an all-out attack on the Egyptian forces in the Sinai desert. The French frankly collaborated with them in this campaign. Israeli parachute troops were dropped by French pilots from French Nord Atlas aircraft. But whatever support Israel received, the attack succeeded beyond all hopes. Israeli troops reached the Suez Canal in four days' fighting.

Then Britain and France issued an ultimatum to Israel and Egypt. Their forces were to withdraw ten miles to east and west of the Canal, or the Anglo-French Forces would intervene. Israel agreed, but Egypt had not yet even acknowledged the ultimatum.

Thus the politics had become complicated. In August when Nasser had grabbed the Canal it had seemed to be simply a question of the soldiers preparing to grab it back again. Now a new situation had arisen which, as it later transpired, was a pity.

Egypt has few natural resources and the Aswan Dam project had stirred up enormous enthusiasm. Arabs are very proud. They felt the snub bitterly when the U.S.A. withdrew the offer of a loan to help towards the Dam. Seizing the Canal was a brilliant move by Nasser. It restored Egyptian amour propre and brought hope that the Dam might yet be financed. Arabs are also businessmen. The Canal to them represented a goldmine, as long as it was in action. No Arab would ever have cut

94

off the western oil supplies on which his gold depended. In Egyptian hands the Canal would work. (As it has, most efficiently, ever since.)

However, to some members of Her Majesty's Government Nasser was a dangerous dictator, to be knocked off his perch. His seizure of the Canal was the Rhineland, Austria and Czechoslovakia all over again.

While 3 PARA was alternately training for war and pursuing EOKA in Cyprus the politicians had not been idle. Negotiations in London, Paris, Cairo and New York had all failed to produce a workable solution to the Suez Canal problem, as the British Government saw it. If the objectives of recovering the Canal to its owners and deposing Nasser were to be achieved there would have to be a recourse to arms. The ponderous military preparations of Britain and France had assembled the gunpowder. Israel lit the fuse.

Tuesday the 30th of October began in the usual way: sick parade, followed by breakfast. Shortly afterwards the Headquarter Company Sergeant Major summoned us to a Company Commander's conference. Sergeant Major Baker was a quietly-spoken courteous man, very unlike the caricature of a Sergeant Major. He had jumped in pitch darkness into the South of France in 1944, and in a 30 m.p.h. wind onto Megera airfield near Athens. He was one of those who had rescued Grivas.

Did he but know it, he was about to do the same for Nasser. For by now, with his Sinai armies smashed by the Israelis, Nasser's hold on his perch was very insecure. Yet we were intervening. To Nasser's heartfelt relief, we were providing him with an excuse for his previous humiliating defeat at the hands of his traditional adversary.

Lawrence Scragg, commanding Headquarter Company, surveyed his officers. We were gathered in his dusty, sparsely furnished office tent. All the departments were represented: signals, motor transport, quartermaster, pay; we got our pencils and notebooks ready. Lawrence savoured the atmosphere of suspense and interest which he had created.

'We are going to load for an Airborne Exercise,' he began. His eye roved over the bunch of us, perched uncomfortably on wooden benches. Then he proceeded to detail loads and distribution of containers to each department.

'Everything's to be packed. Ammunition, water, batteries, medical supplies, just as for an operation. Everything.' Another sweeping glance as we digested this information. It did not need much imagination to see what it all meant. The briefing went on and ended with a round of questions and the final details were confirmed.

'It's just like any other loading exercise,' said Lawrence, bristling slightly, 'but it's got to be right this time.'

The next four days were a nightmare. A hot, dusty wind scourged the camp from end to end, covering everything in a film of cocoa-powder. Notes, clothes, faces, stores, all were tinged the same grubby brown. Meanwhile the routine administration of the camp went on while the battalion prepared for war. Cooking, feeding, washing, pay, entertainment, sick parades and guard duties all had to continue as usual. Most people were packing stores and taking part in two or three different jobs simultaneously. During this chaos Sergeant Rabet was a tower of strength. He supervised the personal packing of all the orderlies, and the more complicated business of filling the cylindrical metal containers with medical stores. These 'C.L.E.' containers, as they were known, were veterans. The design had originated during the war and had not been subsequently modified. No doubt some designs for an improvement were rotting in a file on somebody's desk at the War Office. But 4 'C.L.E.'s' were all we had got. Under the sergeant's keen eye the containers were packed and repacked, the points of balance marked, and the laden weight scrawled in paint beside the Red Crosses on their sides. The orderlies' language was pungent as the huge tin cylinders slipped and rolled onto fingers and toes.

It was not only among the soldiers that distraction reigned. The Second-in-Command of the battalion spent a hectic few

Right:
'To burst … into the torrent of air.' An instructor shows how.

Below:
The battalion with its scattered companies was my first commitment. Cyprus.

Above: 'Red on. Stand in the door.' A stick of the old and bold, with kitbags instead of weapon containers.
Below: The armada of aircraft. Hastings, Valettas and squadrons of Canberras on Nicosia airfield.

CYPRUS

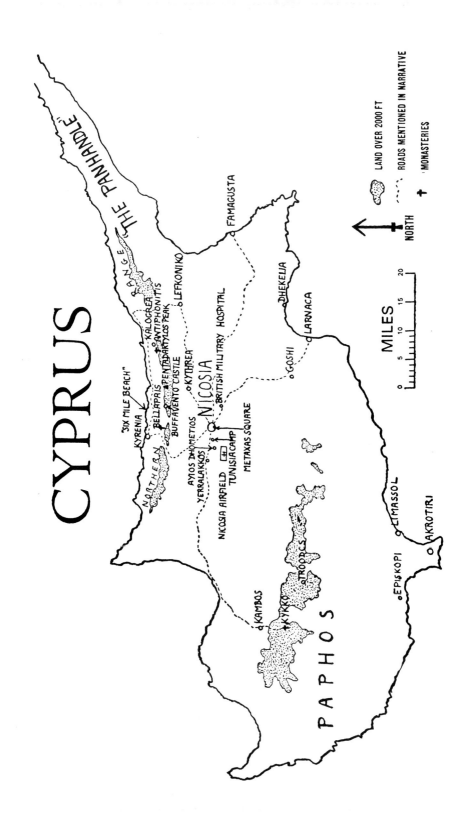

THE PANHANDLE

"SIX MILE BEACH"

KYRENIA
BELLAPAIS
BUFFAVENTO CASTLE
KYTHREA

KALOGREA
ANTIPHONITIS
PENTADAKTYLOS PEAK

NORTHERN   RANGE

LEFKONIKO

NICOSIA
BRITISH MILITARY HOSPITAL

AYIOS DHOMETIOS
YERRALAKKOS
NICOSIA AIRFIELD
TUNIS/A CAMP
METAXAS SQUARE

FAMAGUSTA

GOSHI

DHEKELIA

LARNACA

KAMBOS

KYKKO

TROODOS

P A P H O S

EPISKOPI

LIMASSOL

AKROTIRI

MILES

0   5   10   15   20

NORTH

LAND OVER 2000 FT
ROADS MENTIONED IN NARRATIVE
✝ MONASTERIES

Above: 'The finest soldiers in the world and you don't even know it.' – Noel Hodgson. Awaiting take off in Nicosia.

Opposite
top: Fitting Chutes, November 4th.
bottom: A paratroop sergeant Major checking his men's chutes before taking off from Cyprus.

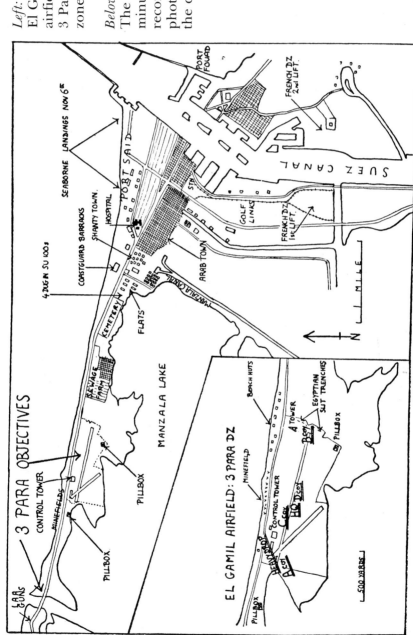

Left:
El Gamil airfield – 3 Para drop zone.

Below:
The last minute reconnaissance photograph of the drop zone.

Above: Granted air support ... anything should prove possible. A Sea Hawk strike on the Coastguard Barracks.
Below: Against the glare of the sun ... the smoke flare ... marked the dropping point.

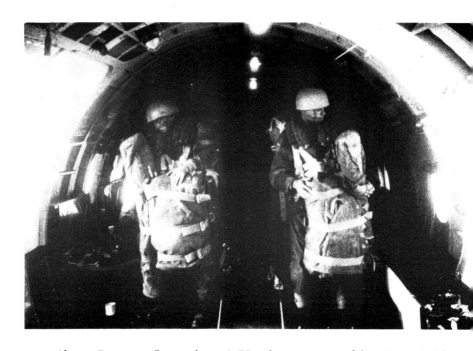

Above: Prepare for action. A Hastings approaching Port Said.
Below: The Hastings were coming in to drop their loads.

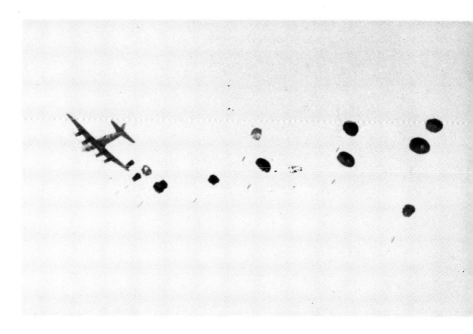

Above: Just like Frensham Common all over again.
Below: The Colonel ... must have missed the runway.

Above:
Ready for whatever
might arrive.

Right:
We did not have to
wait long.

Above: Containers at the west end of the airfield.
Below: In that soft sand the crash pans were intact.

Above: A captured Russian SU 100 dug in, hull down.
Below: The captured SU 100 was driven to the quayside.

Left:
Members of the machine gun platoon. The Colonel had forbidden them from shooting up retreating Egyptians.

Below: A request for helicopter evacuation ... to the Navy offshore. A whirlwind taking off from HMS Albion.

Above: Radfan. A platoon of 'B' Company Group, 3 Para, clearing a line of stone forts in the Wadi Taym.
Below: The first prisoners of the campaign, captured by 'B' Company Headquarters.

Top: The road ... is now a busy dual carriageway.

Left: What they said about the Sims container cannot be printed. A peacetime picture – reserve parachute worn.

days. Major Beckett acted as chief of staff to the Colonel and many administrative details were left in his hands. In addition he must be prepared to take over command should the Colonel become a casualty. He found himself having to decide maddening queries, such as how many pairs of socks each man should carry, and at the same time trying to wind up the Band Account, which was traditionally his concern.

The fiction that this was a loading exercise was short-lived. By the middle of the week two additions to the battalion suggested something more urgent.

The first was a section of the 23rd Parachute Field Ambulance, with three medical officers. Norman Kirby, a major, was in command; bespectacled and balding gently, he wore more the air of a benign physician in a teaching hospital than the parachute-trained surgeon which he was. We had overlapped at Abingdon where he was doing a refresher-course. I had seen a figure in the distance, prepared for jumping, the spectacles glued firmly into place with a bold arrangement of sticking plaster strips. His epaulettes revealed that he was in the Royal Army Medical Corps and we had fallen naturally into conversation. Now I knew more. Norman had dealt personally with many of our surgical problems in Cyprus and had established a bridge between the Field Ambulance and the British Military Hospital, where he worked for most of his time.

His anaesthetist was Malcolm Elliott. Malcolm never failed to surprise. If you met casually you might have thought the tall, angular doctor with prominent cheek-bones and a long forelock was a typical product of A. J. Cronin, doomed to asthenic disaster. Nothing could be further from the truth. Malcolm was always fit, and could play a blinding forehand drive on the tennis court. He had taught me to ride a motor-bike in a spare moment at Aldershot and took an almost masochistic delight in parachuting. In Cyprus he had been dogged by various misfortunes and was frankly pessimistic about the coming operation. But we were later to learn that he had not run out of surprises.

The Battalion Regimental Aid Post, which consisted of medical officer, sergeant, corporal and orderlies was thus heavily reinforced. Norman and Malcolm, with a sergeant and orderlies, constituted our surgical team, prepared to operate on desperate emergencies straightaway. Maurice Fearnley and a section of the Field Ambulance were with us to help with the treatment and evacuation of casualties. Maurice had been a doctor with the Field Ambulance for over a year and knew more about the techniques of moving casualties than the rest of us. In all there were about thirty medical staff with the battalion. Thirty sounds a lot of men to be employed looking after casualties. But none of us expected to be idle.

In the event none of us was.

The other major addition to the battalion were the Sappers. A troop of them were attached to us from 9 Squadron, the Independent Field Squadron of Royal Engineers with the Parachute Brigade. We had got to know '3 Troop' well during our time in Cyprus. Commanded by Captain Brazier, they had accompanied us on several Internal Security operations in the hills. Jock Brazier was wont to sit at the back of the Colonel's conferences or 'O' Groups, when orders were given to all subordinates. Puffing a long slender pipe he appeared to be taking an almost academic interest in what was going on. A few searching questions at the end revealed that nothing had escaped him, and the most practical details were already decided in his mind. His Sappers were a versatile crowd and were equally effective at mixing concrete to floor our medical tent, repairing tumbledown mountain roads or dynamiting EOKA hiding places.

On Thursday, 1st November, the night that the extra troops arrived, the officers of what was now '3 PARA Battalion Group' were bidden to an 'O' Group by the Colonel.

That first briefing was dramatic. We filed into the hut late in the evening. The Colonel and Second-in-Command had come in last.

'If this show is on' Colonel Crook began, 'and it's by no means yet certain that it is, this is the 3 PARA role. We are going to Port Said.' Dead silence.

We were to jump onto El Gamil airfield just to the west of Port Said.

'Fill in the 'I' side, Jim,' the Colonel said. We were gathered in Jim's new palace. A bigger and better hut, more securely shuttered from prying eyes, had been used by the Intelligence Section since our preparations began. Thick coils of Danert wire surrounded the building and an armed guard stood at the door.

Jim Burke strode over to the map of Port Said and began. Enemy forces were sketched in and marked with flags. An armoured division was at large in the desert to the south of us, and considerable mixed forces in Port Said itself. Of more immediate interest, a battalion group surrounded the airfield and some tanks were known to be in the western edge of Port Said, with numerous National Guards to back them up.

In our own private battle we should be outnumbered by five to one.

I sat in comfortable obscurity at the back. At all the Colonel's conferences or 'O' Groups I was an observer rather than a participant. The machine worked and I watched. Conferences were more or less round-table discussions at which the Colonel presided. 'O' or Order Groups were smaller gatherings at which executive orders were given to his company commanders and certain administrative staff. I was privileged in automatically attending both types of gathering. Our briefing was really an 'O' Group. It was all very friendly and christian names were used throughout. But at the same time there was no doubt where the decision of responsibility lay.

'"A" Company with, in support, 3 Troop, 9 Field Squadron . . .' and so it went on. Mike Walsh and his company were to seize the control tower buildings on landing. 'Get in there somehow, Mike.' As the company would land on flat sand and immediately attack the substantial buildings 'somehow' was

99

about it. In all probability heavy fire would be directed at them from the cover of the control tower. When they had overrun the buildings they were to go on to capture the bridge at the west end of the airfield, which the Sappers would prepare for demolition.

'"B" Company, with under command . . .' the faultless routine of orders. Point by point with no omissions. 'B' Company's task initially was the most vital. They had to capture and hold the eastern end of the airfield. Major Stevens was unlikely to allow them to fail in this, or in anything else. Dick Stevens was every inch the professional soldier, tall, lean, fair, with a penetrating glance from his grey eyes. I often felt very small when Dick catechized me on points of medical detail. He was scrupulously fair and the company knew that he would not ask them to do anything which he would not first do himself. The electric light bulbs accentuated the high cheek bones and aquiline nose as Dick absorbed the orders carefully. Not by a flicker did he betray what he thought about it all. His company was to jump last and be dropped within a few yards of prepared Egyptian positions. If anyone had a rough time on landing it would be them.

The briefing was a model of conciseness and clear thinking. In forty minutes the disposition of the battalion and the battle we were to fight was all made clear. An extra 'D' Company of what were known as 'employed men' was to be formed. These were the various cooks, clerks, storemen and orderlies who, up till the last moment, would be administering the camp. Once on the ground they were to collect near the control tower buildings, and form a reserve force to help clear the airfield and provide reinforcements where necessary. Major Hodgson was to be in command, a welcome change for Noel from his duties as 'P.R.I.'

'Make sure that everybody hits the ground where they want to be,' was the Colonel's directive to the Air Adjutant. Now it was up to Captain Howlett to arrange that it was so.

Geoffrey Howlett shared the dusty, distracting office tent of

Gerald Mullins. The exasperating business of air travel in all its forms was his concern. That included synthetic training, aircraft drill, loading of aircraft with containers, 'Heavy-Drop', and men, and transporting men and equipment to and from the airfield. He was always at it. If an aircraft went unserviceable or 'u/s' or the weather ruled out parachuting all the chaos of cancellation, alteration and mutilation of existing plans fell on him. The move of the battalion by air back to England had been a prolonged anxiety. 'Heavy Drop' was a headache in itself.

Now, I am told, things are a little better. At that time, if our lives had not depended on it, the equipment situation would have been comic.

The basic army vehicle was the Champ, a wonderfully sprung quarter-ton truck, with a waterproofed Rolls-Royce engine; it could not be 'crated-up' to be carried with parachutes under the belly of a Hastings on account of its weight. So seven old Jeeps were conjured up, souvenirs of the war probably. These, duly crated, were to be slung beneath Hastings aircraft for the flight to Port Said. When the dropping-point was reached they would fall away. From each would blossom four enormous parachutes to land, with not more than a good thump, at the west end of El Gamil airfield. That was if the release apparatus and the parachutes worked. Neither were entirely reliable.

Our whole defence against tanks depended on those Jeeps and their loads. A sort of keen anticipation swept the officers mess after the initial briefing. Nothing very tangible, but the atmosphere had changed. Bill Hill, the lieutenant in command of the anti-tank platoon, was looking forward to his task more enthusiastically than most. The '106' which his platoon had mastered so efficiently was about to be proved.

But the '106' had never been dropped by parachute. At short notice the versatile firm of Tri-ang had concocted a monster metal cylinder which held two guns secure, packed in giant-sized corrugated cardboard. What they thought, in

1956, about beating their Kiddy-cars into weapon-containers is not recorded. But the soldiers appreciated it.

Three of these huge tin cans were to be suspended beneath Hastings aircraft. There were also trailers for four of the Jeeps. For better or worse the 'Heavy Drop' was complete. It remained to be seen whether it all reached the ground intact. Much depended on the thoroughness of the soldiers who crated it up for dropping. Metal crash-pans would be lashed beneath the wheels of the transport to cushion the shock of landing. The huge parachutes would be firmly shackled on. Six of the precious guns were to fly with us.

President Eisenhower had just roundly condemned Operation *Musketeer*, as the Anglo-French Intervention was known. He would have been galled to know how entirely the spearhead of the attack on Egypt depended on those six American '106's'.

My driver Smith was one of the lucky few in the M.T. Platoon detailed to fly in the first lift of aircraft. Their duty was to uncrate the Jeeps from their crash pans and parachutes, and to make sure they were delivered to the drivers of the anti-tank guns. Whatever happened the anti-tank guns must get into the right positions. Once they were safely placed the Jeeps could be used for less essential tasks, like carrying ammunition, stores, and casualties. Unless they reached their positions there was a chance that casualties would be their only freight. One or two well-organised Russian tanks on the edge of the airfield . . .

The remainder of the M.T. Platoon were to leave Cyprus by sea. Bitterly disappointed, they watched their friends prepare to drop in the first major parachute operation since 1945. But they and the members of the 'Second lift' which was to follow us eight hours later in the day helped us to the last.

Not until Saturday, 3rd November, did the soldiers know the details of what was planned. The operation at that stage was due to begin on Tuesday the sixth. When the Colonel briefed the battalion the officers had a fair idea of what was to come.

What we could not anticipate was the audience reaction as the Colonel took his soldiers into his confidence. The battalion was assembled in the big Nissen hut. Camp was sealed, and the doors were guarded.

'From now on,' he said, 'security is vital to us all.' Absolute silence. He walked across to a veiled blackboard. 'A careless word from one of you after this may endanger all our lives.' The silence thickened. 'When you are asked to sign for a parachute over at the airfield tomorrow don't say 'I'll sign for it in Port Said' because that's where we're going.'

The Intelligence Officer unveiled the blackboard, revealing the map of Port Said pinned to it.

'There's Port Said. And that's the airfield.' Studied pause. 'That's what I want you to capture.'

Prolonged silence. Then from the middle of the crowd a flat, small, clear voice:

'Thank you!'

Someone, I think it was the R.S.M., barked: 'Silence!' But the Colonel went on imperturbably. This sort of thing had become part of his relationship with his men. He told them all he possibly could.

'There's the main runway,' he said as he finished his briefing, 'and I expect to hit it very hard.' Howls of laughter.

The Colonel fully loaded weighed about fourteen stone and his parachute landings were something of a legend.

'Thank you' was just about it. As they absorbed the information the battalion were grateful. Within themselves everyone was glad. Not that they underestimated what was coming. The thought of landing on the open airfield under fire was hard to stifle. But they were glad to have been chosen to do it, glad to do something positive at last. For a soldier's profession is unlike any other. He spends a lot of time training, learning to fight, and all the time a large part of him hopes he will never have to do so. His whole effort is made within this proviso. And when the order finally comes it is a relief. The dilemma is resolved. It is all going to be justified.

A lot needed justification. Eleven years of marching, jumping, packing, firing, moving and training lay behind. Only the
old and bold among us could remember all that had gone
between the crossing of the Rhine in 1945 and November 1956.
But all the men had memories of months or years getting ready
for this.

Now it was time to pay attention to our personal loads.
Everyone had much to carry. Small kit, ammunition, water
bottles, and rations in addition to their own weapons. Each
man was also carrying extra mortar bombs or machine-gun
ammunition. All this had to be packed into our individual
canvas weapon-containers for jumping.

'Why not take a Bergen, sir?' Colour Bradley asked. Any
offer of kit from any army store should be immediately taken
up. Such chances are rare.

But it had been decided that 'war-time accounting' should
hold sway during Operation *Musketeer*. And all stores had
become surprisingly generous in consequence. I accepted the
Colour Sergeant's offer of a Bergen rucksack. Its capacious dark
interior would hold all my odds and ends in comfort. Saline,
instruments, dressings, morphia, water, rations, all piled in
very tidily. It weighed nearly a hundred pounds and I could
only just lift it. The frame of the Bergen poked out of my
weapon-container and I attempted to mask it with Elastoplast.
It must not get caught up.

The Regimental Aid Post was probably as well equipped as
it could be. Certainly between us we could have carried very
little more into battle. The orderlies carrying stretchers had
the most awkward loads. The Airborne stretcher is a master-
piece of lightness and portability, but when folded and stowed
it is still about four feet long and uncomfortably bulky. The
sergeant was going to carry a stretcher and the most immense
weapon-container 'just in case'.

Both he and the corporal had spent several years in the
Canal Zone before Britain had handed it over to Egypt. They
took my personal packing firmly in hand.

'These Gippo bastards don't respect the Red Cross,' they said. 'You put a weapon in your pocket, sir, and have it handy.' The 9 mm. Browning automatic pistol would bulge ominously in the left-hand pocket of my smock. I was not happy about either the ethics or the safety of having it there. We wore small Red Cross armlets on our right arms. It did indeed seem unlikely that an Egyptian, faced by an airborne invasion of his homeland, would credit the armlet even if he noticed it. By the Geneva Convention Medical Officers are only permitted to use weapons in self-defence. When you are taking part in a flagrant act of aggression where does self-defence begin? Safety was a more immediate matter. I had taken the trouble to master the elements of loading and firing the pistol on the range. It was surprisingly difficult to be accurate with it. My respect for the gunmen in films, who shoot people dead with one shot at thirty yards, has risen a lot since I tried it myself. But details of the safety catch and cocking handle were more difficult still. When you stopped firing the gun remained cocked and loaded unless the magazine was exhausted. The lightest pressure on the trigger would set it off. Later this nearly proved my undoing.

Holden, my batman, was not to be outdone where my personal safety was concerned. On Friday morning he came into my tent.

'These are for you, sir,' and he spilled out an armful of grenades, smoke-bombs and plastic explosive.

'For God's sake, Holden, I shall only have an accident with that lot. Give it away to someone who knows how to use it.' And he went away, crestfallen, to dispose of it among his numerous friends in the Drums Platoon.

Time was getting short. The dusty wind still blew. The metal containers, loaded for war, were driven over to the airfield to be 'bombed up' on the armada of transport aircraft waiting to take us to Port Said. 'The armada of aircraft' sounds impressive. As a description of twenty-seven part-worn Valettas, carrying twenty men, and Hastings, carrying thirty, it is scarcely accurate. But it represented the entire available transport force of R.A.F. Transport Command.

And that night one of them went u/s. To someone like myself, who can seldom start a lawn-mower, the ease with which an aircraft 'goes u/s' is not surprising. This particular Valetta was carrying a lot of our combined medical supplies in a metal container slung beneath the wings. We brought the container back to camp from the airfield. Gloomily the doctors stood around the 300-pound cylinder, deciding what was essential and which stores could be left to come over by re-supply. Plaster-of-paris bandages and shell-dressings in their waterproof packs littered the parade ground. The remainder went to swell our individual weapon-containers.

*   *   *

The sense of distraction increased as time ran out. Our work was punctuated by the shriek of Hunter aircraft taking off overhead in pairs every hour to patrol the sky above Cyprus. At dusk and in the hours before dawn our rest or recreation was shattered by the sky-tearing roar of the Canberra squadrons taking off to bomb the Egyptian runways.

It seemed far from certain that the operation would occur at all, when we heard of the political uproar at home which reached us via the B.B.C. news bulletins. But no dissent permeated the ranks of 3 PARA. The Colonel was amused at the suggestions in the press that his soldiers, disagreeing with the politics of the operation, might refuse to carry it out. The better the soldier the better he obeys his orders. And Colonel Crook knew his soldiers were very good indeed. That was not the point, though. It was not a question of his ordering and men obeying. The battalion was a unit. If 3 PARA was ordered to capture an airfield in Egypt, 3 PARA would do so or else. . . . To refuse, or opt out of something which the battalion was going to do would simply not cross any one's mind.

For the politics, the rights and wrongs of the operation were no concern of 3 PARA. They were soldiers, trained to obey, and now given a job to do. The general feeling was of satisfaction that Nasser was about to be taught a lesson.

Perhaps Horace and I were the only ones who had voiced our doubts, and that only to each other. Horace, the padre, was attached to us in the middle of the week. He shared my tent and we had talked a lot. I had come to know Horace well during my eight weeks in Cyprus, though he normally lived with I PARA in the adjoining camp. Horace and I sat on our beds, surveying the chaos of equipment which we were trying to pack. With great speed he bundled his blackthorn walking stick into the weapon sleeve of his container. His prayer book, cross and communion set were gone in a flash, and his small kit completed the load.

'Can I take anything for you?'

I off-loaded various dressings and a bottle or two.

'I can't believe all this is right, can you?' I said. We talked round it all ways. This cold-blooded attack on a weaker country, for whatever ends, did not fit in. Fair play, a nation of shopkeepers, gentlemen's agreements, all the Church and medicine stood for, was something apart from this. We took a rather weak-minded comfort from the fact that we personally were non-combatants, and our first duty was to our own congregation and patients. We were accessories before, during and after the fact for all that.

When our personal packing was almost finished, we did a furious session of 'synthetic' training. We practised rolls on some very hard mats, and exits from a makeshift dummy fuselage. Then over to the airfield where we performed Aircraft Drill under the vigilant eye of a Royal Air Force Sergeant Instructor. The stick of parachutists emplanes in the reverse order to that of jumping. Corporal Dunbavin and I had difficulty working out which side of the aircraft we were to sit. The Valetta, sitting on the tarmac in the midday sun on Nicosia airfield was like an oven. Three times we swopped places in our confusion, and the Royal Air Force Sergeant was exasperated. 'The Aircraft Drill's very important,' I had overheard a senior officer from Brigade Headquarters say that morning. He had survived, despite being shot down on the way to Arnhem, so he ought to know. Eventually we got it right, to everyone's relief.

Throughout the battalion preparations were almost complete. Each company and department had packed, checked and weighed its kit. Whatever happened nothing would be left to chance. In the twenty seconds we expected the transport aircraft to spend covering the Dropping Zone there would be no time to waste on chances.

The state of the D.Z., as a Dropping Zone is usually known, was of immediate importance. The Intelligence Section kept analysing the air reconnaissance photographs as they came in. Since Jim Burke's impressive display of knowledge at the initial briefing of the officers we had placed great faith in his organisation.

Jim later admitted that lifemanship played a big part in his original exposition. Much of the information he required simply did not exist. Considering that Egypt was still infested by unfortunate British subjects, this was surprising.

Jim had even been to the G.H.Q. of the whole operation at Episkopi on the south coast of the Island in his search for facts, but he returned with his hopes once more dashed.

Perhaps this had given him a more light-hearted view of the operation than some of us. He also had packed a Bergen rucksack, vowing that whatever befell he would be comfortable in Egypt. Into it he crammed several changes of clothing, a thousand cigarettes, several books, playing cards, writing materials, two large rolls of toilet paper, pyjamas 'and a host of other, totally useless items'.

But any excesses Jim might make would be counterbalanced by his sergeant. Sergeant Sparvell had taken part in too many quick moves of the battalion for alleged political crises to be over-impressed by this one. But he was thorough. For hours at a time during the last few days he had been poring over the air reconnaissance photographs of El Gamil airfield. Most of his conclusions were about to be vindicated.

The marked maps from which we had been briefed, the lists of Egyptian forces, silhouettes of Russian aircraft and armour which might be encountered, were prepared by the Intelligence Section. Under Jim's direction Sergeant Sparvell personally supervised every detail in the assembly and production of their material. If we did not know much about what to expect when we hit the ground it was no fault of theirs.

The uncertainty of it all seemed to leave most men untouched. They had all been well briefed. Company commanders had briefed their platoon commanders who had gone over the battle again and again with their men using maps and air photographs. Whatever opposition they encountered, each man knew what he had to do.

That evening another distraction loomed. We received the news that the operation had been brought forward 24 hours to Monday, the 5th November. 3 PARA would be leading the way, which pleased everyone. Less pleasing was the news that a Sapper had been injured while 'bombing up' containers on the airfield. He had been previously briefed for the operation. If he were given an anaesthetic in hospital anything might leak out. We rushed off, to find him safely enclosed in a sealed ward.

We could have saved ourselves the trouble. We knew some of the background of the operation: that we were one of the few British armies to have taken to the field in recent history in the knowledge that our country was divided behind us; that Parliament was in an uproar about the merits of the action we were about to take. We did not know that the dubious political object of conserving our enemies' lives was being achieved by imperilling our own. For this was exactly what was going on. The bombing of the Egyptian runways in the phoney ultimatum period was fair enough. A few Mig fighters at large in our air armada would have wrought havoc. So was the web of security woven around our objectives. What was less easy to understand was the limitation of the bombardment in our own particular area, chiefly because the operation had been brought forward. Most incredible of all was the warning to civilians to keep clear of the beach area in Port Said. This was broadcast over Cyprus Radio that night.

Had we all known about this we would have laughed at our efforts to maintain security.

On Sunday, 4th November the wind which had scoured our week of preparation dropped. The parade ground dust was stilled and the maroon flag, with the wings and battle honours, drooped flabbily from the pole above us. The battalion was holding a drumhead service. In a close square the companies were formed up around the dais on which Horace stood. The tight-packed rows of young sunburned faces looked unwontedly serious. We were not a religious crowd I suppose. But not many crowds are. In his address Horace read some lines of Studdert-Kennedy's. From *Woodbine Willie* of the 1914–18 war, I suspect, Horace had learnt much of his easy, frank, uncomplicated approach to the Toms and to all of us. Towards the end of the service he said the Airborne Forces Prayer.

May the defence of the Most High be above and beneath, around and within us, in our going out and our coming in, in our rising up and our going down, all our days and all our nights until the dawn when the Sun of Righteousness shall arise with healing in His Wings for the people of the world, through Jesus Christ our Lord. Amen.

There was a pause. The steep sunlight leant down on the silent crowd. How many of us would there be next time? And what sort of service would we be holding? Eventually we dispersed and the groups returning to their tents were uncommonly subdued. Our anaesthetist Malcolm Elliott later wondered 'how the Padre could give us God's blessing and the rest of it I don't know.'

Probably we needed it more than anyone else that day. It may have been only the doctors and padres in the Brigade who had their doubts. Certainly they were the only people who could afford to air them, either then or later. For a soldier has to serve two Deities, and if it comes to a showdown Orders will take precedence over God or Conscience. '*Befehl ist Befehl.*' Orders are Orders, the cry of the S.S., the N.K.V.D. and also, in less extreme conditions, the cry of all soldiers in all wars, always. Normally in a British army one hopes there will be no conflict between the two Deities.

But very little about Operation *Musketeer* was normal.

The Toms were fortunately ignorant of most of this. Even had they known, it would have made no difference now. If their C.O. said the airfield was to be captured, that was it. No matter how many something Gippos were waiting for them. No matter what the Labour Party said about it. It had been nearly as funny as the 'Goon Show', the news lately. And the 'Goon Show' had sustained us for many months now. Very often episodes in the campaign against EOKA might have been lifted straight from Spike Milligan's script. Much of Operation *Musketeer* was in similar vein.

It was a busy Sunday. The afternoon was devoted to rehearsal. Each stick of parachutists was driven over to the airfield in a chalk-numbered truck to the corresponding chalk-numbered aircraft waiting on the perimeter track. We pushed our absurdly heavy personal containers out of the truck and laid them in neat lines on the dusty ground. Sergeant Crompton of 'A' Company, our stick commander, examined each one minutely. The fifteen-foot nylon suspension-cords were coiled neatly and tied into their sockets with thread. On these nylon cords the containers would eventually hang below us as we neared the ground at Port Said. The suspension hooks were checked. These tether the container tightly onto the parachute harness until, with a flick with your thumbs, you let it jerk away to hang clear on the cord. The leg straps were checked. They serve to keep the container tight against your body as you struggle towards the door of the aircraft and out into the slipstream. Before the container can be dropped clear the legstrap must be freed by pulling a quick-release pin. Any rust on the pin may make it jam, and I had lubricated mine with butter from the mess dining tent. 'It's got to be right this time.'

Then we collected the parachute packs off our seats in the aircraft and fitted them outside, adjusting the buckles of the harness so that each strap was a snug, symmetrical fit. After this the parachutes were taken off and replaced on our seats. The weapon containers were stacked in the aisle down the centre of the aircraft. Everything was ready.

In camp that evening time began to hang heavy. A small ginger kitten had adopted the tent which I shared with Horace as its temporary home. Cats usually shun me as if I were an Alsatian, and this seemed a poor omen. So when Malcolm and Norman suggested we went to the Military Hospital I was glad to join them. They were picking up one or two after-thoughts in the way of equipment, and also our precious small supply of blood for transfusion. This had been kept in the refrigerator there until the last moment. Blood must not be warmed long before it is transfused; but we expected to use the blood very soon now. We seemed an uncouth bunch walking the clean corridors and operating theatres in boots and smocks. The theatre sisters, who had become firm friends of Norman and Malcolm during the last few weeks were nearly in tears. They knew what the visit meant.

Back in camp the busiest people from now on would be the Rear Party. All our personal belongings were crated up in the Quartermaster's stores. Although the battalion was leaving camp, much equipment in the way of accommodation stores would remain behind. The Rear Party were responsible for safeguarding the camp and its stores and eventually for handing it over to some unspecified occupants. After this they were to rejoin the battalion as soon as possible in Egypt. The Rear Party Commander was equal to his task: Major Edwards, our paymaster, could easily handle the morass of administrative detail involved and bundle his party on the first available transport to Port Said. With Ted in command and Bob Grainger at his right hand we need have no worries about our belongings

back in Cyprus. To his chagrin Bob had been deputed to the
Rear Party, while his R.Q.M.S. Chippy was about to jump
with the battalion. How many hundred jumps he had done I
didn't dare ask. He had been on one of the earlier parachute
courses during the war, at Ringway. Parachute failures in
those days were regrettably frequent.

'I remember watching a stick out of a Whitley,' Chippy had
said. 'Number 3 had a Candle.' The unopened parachute
trailing behind a man falling to his death was known as a
'Roman Candle'.

'We went across to pick up the body and found he'd fallen
into a marsh in a wood. There he was, up to his armpits in
mud and water, cursing like hell. He wasn't surprised to be
alive. He was just angry with the R.A.F. for dropping him in
such a rotten place. The branches and mud had broken his
fall.'

We should have no branches or mud to contend with, if all
went well. But, however badly it turned out, Chippy was sure
to have seen worse.

The short night was gone. At 0115 hours on Monday we
were up for breakfast, the most insipid meal I have ever tasted.
Then 'Chalk 7' reassembled by the truck which was to take
us away. It was final. This was the end of an episode. Irrele-
vant details were suddenly important. The telephone post
beside the truck, bruised dried pine, it was now a permanency
here compared with ourselves. We had made early starts
before, but this morning we were doing it all for the last time.
The padded footfall of rubber-soled boots, the hoarse purring
of the three-tonner engines and, above all, the smells were
nostalgic. Sage, lime, alkaline dust, resin from some distant
pines, all compounded into the redolence of Cyprus. Cutting
across this were our own smells, sweat, webbing equipment,
rifle oil, exhaust fumes. The two were incompatible, as we
were with Cyprus. We were mere birds of passage.

Back once more by the aircraft the stick prepared to emplane.
Someone conjured up a drink of cocoa. Figures clumped off

into the dark to make water. We checked our helmets under Sergeant Crompton's gruff supervision. Just like that squad on 'P' course again, but there was less ribaldry this time. The sergeant called the nominal roll. Everyone was present.

'Before we emplane I have to warn you that the green light constitutes an order to jump.'

CHAPTER VII

THROUGH THE GREAT WIDE AIR

W E received the sergeant's ritual caution in silence. Just as the policeman warns his suspect that anything he says may be taken down . . . so the stick commander warns his stick that the green light . . .

In the cosy gloom of the aircraft it suddenly became a small war. The great preparations were over, it was a business of sticks of a mere 20 or 30 men until we met up with the rest of the battalion on the ground at Port Said.

We were a varied crowd in the Valetta drawn from every branch of the Battalion Group. All of the transport aircraft carried similar polyglot loads. 'A' Company formed the front part of each stick and 'B' Company the rear. 'A' Company were to clear and hold the west end of the airfield, 'B' Company the east end, 'C' Company were to form a reserve in the middle, after clearing the south edge facing the lagoon. Support and Headquarters Companies were also fitted into the middle of each stick. Their task was to concentrate near the control tower buildings after 'A' Company had cleared the enemy from them. All the hangers-on, the medical staff, sappers and gunners were allocated to Headquarter Company.

We picked our way uncertainly over the weapon-containers stacked in the gangway and found our seats. The Captain of the aircraft came aft to address us. The aircrew wore flak-suits and it all seemed to be in deadly earnest.

'We shall fly at eight hundred feet over the sea and come down to six hundred to drop you,' he said. 'I'll cut the slipstream down as much as possible over the Dropping Zone.'

In the dim interior lighting he seemed surprisingly young to have all this responsibility as he ran over the flight plan and met. reports. 'You've had the ditching drill explained? Good luck.'

And we settled back in our seats, loosening our helmets. The flight would last about two hours and we might as well be comfortable. It was a moment of relief shared by the whole battalion.

Distraction was gone, calculations, preparations, reservations—all were behind us now. All we needed now was twenty good steps to the door and a clean exit when the time came. That would be enough.

After a long trundle round the perimeter track the Valetta turned to face down the runway. The pilot warmed his engines carefully and opened the throttles wide. We sagged backwards in our seats as the speed built up. After a very long run we were airborne, drooped low over the lights of Tunisia Camp, and turned away south for Egypt.

Each man was wrapped in the cocoon of his own thoughts. Many of the Toms slept. Noel Hodgson who was to command 'D' Company marvelled as he stared at the snoring figures. Chin straps loosened and helmets perched on the backs of their heads. The wonderful capacity of the British Tom for sleep. There you are, he thought, the finest soldiers in the world and you don't even know it.

For they were. To their officers, and among themselves they were always The Toms, just the latest in line of generations of amateur soldiers. But no one whose ancestors have at one time or another fought most of the nations in the world can be quite unmilitary. If you select a bunch of such men for their determination and aggressiveness, train them hard, give them tough and experienced leaders, and the best available equipment—even the best that a short-sighted, parsimonious treasury will provide—if you do all this then the result is bound to be extraordinary. A parachute battalion. This was the finished product, ready to go. Soon it would be poised, like the sword of Damocles, over the heads of the hapless defenders of Port Said.

The patchy, irregular, frustrating struggle against EOKA had done much to 3 PARA. Much for it as well. The sticks of parachutists approaching Port Said were more now than just a well-selected and fit unit. They were hard. The months of hot, alert days, alarms, tragedies, had left their mark. I had entered the story late and was little more than a surf-rider on the battalion wave. And, like a surfer, I knew that once the wave of bodies packed in the Valetta started to break out of the door I should be swept along with them.

It was inevitable.

The sword was about to fall. Yet the Toms did not think of themselves as extraordinary in any way. Nor individually were they. At heart most of them were civilians, the reservists more recently so than the rest. Private Penning of 'C' Company spent the flight swamped with homesickness for the life he had just left. Back at home in Enfield the bride he had married two months ago would not yet even be awake. How far away it all seemed. They had married by special licence three days before leaving for Cyprus. . . . He dozed off and the flight seemed to take no time at all.

Geoff Norton felt nothing but relief. As Support Company Commander he had spent a harrowing few days calculating the numbers and weights of the various ammunition his company needed; for Vickers guns, '106's' and mortars. There were four 3-inch mortars, and about 150 bombs for each mortar. That should be enough for a day's fighting. He was glad that the discussions and decisions were over. The unreal atmosphere of our departure, the sticks of parachutists loading and emplaning in the semi-darkness of Nicosia airfield had made him feel detached, apart. The wrench of parting from his wife and two small boys in their bungalow in the village near the camp, all this was behind. Now it was simple. Get onto the ground and help his platoon commanders do their jobs.

Jim Burke, the Intelligence Officer, had been hard at it to

the end, right until we climbed into trucks in camp to drive
to the airfield. He had been responsible for bringing in the last-
minute air reconnaissance photographs of the D.Z., showing
that the Sapper's bridge had already been destroyed by bombing, and that numerous small black objects in neat lines had
appeared over El Gamil in the last few days. Someone had
suggested to the Commanding Officer that these were a new
form of electrically detonated mine. The Colonel did not pass
this information on to his troops. Sergeant Sparvell, after
hours of intensive poring over the pictures with a powerful lens,
had concluded that these black specks might prove to be empty
40-gallon oil drums.

The dark sky faded gradually as we flew south. It would soon
be daylight. Alternately I dozed and read *The Lonely Road* by
Nevil Shute, surely the gloomiest book he ever wrote. Then
my neighbour nudged me and pointed out of the window. It
was dawn and below us on the grey sea the fleet steamed for
Port Said. We were beating the gunboats to it.

The Colonel must have had many anxieties at the back of
his mind as his Valetta approached the Dropping Zone. They
were not obvious to his companions. He spent the flight
immersed in a thriller topically entitled *Crook's Travels* which
he later threw, with evident satisfaction, into the slipstream.
But for a Commanding Officer he had not been well informed
on a number of important details. The inscrutable web of
politics surrounding Operation *Musketeer* was to blame for most
of this obscurity. And when, two days ago, the operation had
all been brought forward twenty-four hours, it meant that the
Naval bombardment planned to cover our arrival would not
be available. The ships below us would still be a day's sailing
away in the Mediterranean when we arrived at Port Said. Our
air support was an uncertain quantity. We were going in
very much alone, and entirely dependent on wireless for any
help at all.

Now the wirelesses were all packed, on men or in trailers.
A number of spare sets were coming too. Valves and batteries

do not readily withstand the shock of landing. And a battalion without its signals is about as co-ordinated as a man who has had a stroke. The nervous system is missing. Much of the Arnhem disaster might have been avoided had wireless communications been more effective.

Whatever happened Port Said was unlikely to turn into another Arnhem, where the battle had lasted for more than a week. The problem for 3 PARA was to last an hour, a few minutes even: time enough to get off the Dropping Zone under fire. If we could do that all would be well.

Granted air support of the quality we had witnessed in Cyprus, anything should prove possible. Those deadly pinpointed rocket attacks were fresh in everyone's memory and provided that our few wirelesses worked properly, this was the sort of support we could expect over Port Said. But there had been complications even with this arrangement, for the Royal Air Force fighters were not available. Port Said was too near the limit of their range from Cyprus. A jet fighter at low altitude drinks a great deal of fuel and must preferably operate near its base. So we were under the mantle of the Fleet Air Arm and were depending on the help of aircraft from carriers somewhere at sea between Cyprus and Egypt.

Most of us were ignorant of the big problems surrounding us. Penning and the boys in his stick never gave them a thought. A despatcher had offered them all a swig of whisky halfway over. Penning couldn't face it, but gave a double ration to his neighbour. He could have sworn the man staggered a little as they formed up later on. The Tom's thoughts may not have ranged very far. Each man had his own anxieties of home or family, but now all this was forgotten. The coming jump demanded all the concentration he could muster. Each understood his own part in the battle exactly.

'Prepare for action!' The shouted instruction brought us all to our feet as the Despatchers lifted off the door. The webbing strops were run along the cable and we hooked our

static lines to them. A last look as we tightened the parachute harnesses, slotting the lugs of each strap into the
release boxes on our chests. 'Stick stand up.' And we hitched
on the ponderous weapon containers, hooking them on to
the parachute harnesses, fastening the suspension cords
to our waist-bands, tightening the leg straps. We were
ready.

Another shout, and we made sure. Finally we 'told off'.

'Twenty okay.' 'Nineteen okay.' 'Eighteen okay.' And
so on down the stick. Slapping the shoulder of the man in front,
bellowing at the top of our voices against the roar of the engines
and the hissing blast of the slipstream in the doorway. The
Despatchers re-checked us and nursed us into position. Human
error had been virtually eliminated. The infallible X-type
parachute could be relied on to get us safely onto the ground at
Port Said. As we were to jump from 600 feet without reserve
parachutes, this was just as well.

The reserve parachute is a recent development. Britain only
adopted it in 1955 to conform with N.A.T.O. practice. It is
always worn in training, but abandoned on operations to cut
down weight and bulk inside the overloaded and overcrowded
aircraft. I felt bereft without it.

Without a reserve parachute it was more important than
ever to make a good exit. The immediate problem was to keep
close-packed as we followed Sergeant Crompton out of the
door, and keep a compact position when the slipstream hit us.
From six hundred feet our descent would take less than half a
minute. No time to mess about getting out of twists. Lowering
our equipment away and preparing to land would fill all the
precious seconds.

All of us were feeling the same thing. The apprehension of an
impending jump. For it is always the same. Knowledge may
dispel fear, the uncontrollable ignorant fear which renders
people useless. No amount of knowledge or experience can
remove that hollow-gutted awareness of what is coming.
Adrenaline and the 'fight or flight reaction' is how the physio-

THROUGH THE GREAT WIDE AIR

logists dismiss it. But I doubt whether the professor who coined the phrase had parachute soldiers in mind.

It was folding up the seats which produced most adrenaline from Number 2 in the stick and myself. Those seats! They folded up in groups of five and were then secured with a hook. Our lot had jammed. With them down we should never get out. For an ugly moment we wrestled in vain and then they came free. Nothing should go wrong now.

'Red on. Stand in the door!'

Sergeant Crompton edged forward. The slipstream tore at his smock.

It had been a long eleven months since that breakfast at St. Thomas's. 'Dustbins and smelly feet.' Better than this. 'Who is the boss of Suez.' That was the Christmas Show two years ago. Sam Thomas dressed up as Farouk, in a Fez and dark glasses. 'Got to be right this time.'

It was still right today. I checked the Corporal's strop again and edged my left foot forward to ease the weight a little. Surreptitiously my right hand fingered the release-box of the parachute harness. Let that come undone at six hundred feet and . . . Don't be a fool. You've already checked it three times and so has the despatcher. How much longer can they expect us to stand here like this?

At six hundred feet, straight and level, the Valetta flew into the eye of the rising sun. Our ears strained for the pregnant revving of engines which precedes the green light. This is produced by altering the propellers into fine pitch. Rather like changing down in a car, it enables the pilot to control his height and accelerate easier. He is perilously near stalling speed when dropping parachutists. If he stalls, the aircraft falls out of the sky like a brick.

We did not know then how much hard practice had been necessary. Nor, as the final stage of the run-in began, did we know that the pilot was straining his eyes beneath a makeshift visor. Against the overwhelming glare of the sun he was picking up the smoke flare which marked the dropping point. A low-flying Canberra bomber had dropped this a few minutes earlier.

One way and another there was a good deal we did not know.

'Conditions over the Egyptian coast are ideal,' the pilot had said as we emplaned. 'Wind speed zero to five knots and good visibility.' I looked out of the window. The visibility was beyond doubt. The wind I couldn't guess. El Gamil Airfield was six hundred yards wide and bounded by sea to the north and a lagoon to the south. The forecast had better be right.

Two months ago that battalion jump at Imber had been the dress-rehearsal. The cast had not reappeared on stage until today. For 'Stage' in the form of aircraft and parachutes had not existed in Cyprus. There had been enough of each for the drop by 'C' Company in mid-September. Otherwise our airborne training had been simulated. Trucks had scattered the various elements of the battalion over large areas of the dusty Cyprus plough, complete with our weapon-containers. Every man understood the drill for rallying and leaving the Dropping Zone perfectly. Nevertheless it had not always worked like clockwork. Now we were to be scattered over a larger area of Egypt from the air. Each of us knew his objective on landing. Rallying as such had been cut to a minimum, for everyone expected to be fighting the moment he hit the ground.

I was half expecting the Valetta to be hit by anti-aircraft fire. I had watched a number of aircraft trundling over Dropping Zones shedding their loads of parachutists. They flew so slowly and so low that even an Egyptian ack-ack gunner should be able to hit a few. Perhaps by the time Chalk 7 appeared overhead they would have got their eye in. I remembered what Rob had told me of the sudden great holes in his Dakota at Arnhem.

Nobody else seemed in the least concerned.

I looked at the sand bar through the window. Egypt.

Pharaohs. Nasser. I wished this was a night jump. It might then turn out less like a shooting gallery with ourselves as targets.

The red light shone for ages, and we began to wilt under our loads. Stay alert. Anyone slow to move when the time came might not live to regret it. One out of the twenty of us could expect to get hit anyway, so Norman Kirby had told us when the doctors had held a sombre little conference among themselves yesterday. Six per cent casualties were anticipated in the first twenty-four hours. The Battalion Group, consisting of 3 PARA, an attachment of Sappers, gunners, two R.A.F. personnel and one Frenchman, came to nearly 600 men. The medical staff would all be quite busy.

The green light flashed. Sergeant Crompton and the next two men had jumped before I realised it. Left-right, left-right, I hustled after the Corporal towards the doorway. The long flight from Cyprus was over.

Left-right, left-right, left-right. The left foot is in the lead all the time if you are to jump out of the port door of an aircraft, the right shuffles along behind it. Our steps were tiny and tentative. It was vital not to trip or fall. With all that equipment on us recovery would be impossible. I was getting near the door, the Corporal's static line in the palm of my left hand. Important not to drop it now. Most of the stick had gone. Most of our twenty seconds over the Dropping Zone had gone too. Hurry to catch up. Left-right. Drop the static line. Left. Hand round the edge of the door. Right! Into the fanning warmth of the slipstream, and falling away, spiralling, into the mother-of-pearl Egyptian dawn.

We were not the only people parachuting onto Port Said that morning. A few miles away to the south-east were the French. A battalion of them were jumping onto an uncomfortably small Dropping Zone near the Ferdan bridge. The bridge carries the main road south from Port Said over a large channel leading into the Lake Manzala from the main Suez Canal. This was the French objective. Once it was safely in their hands no

Egyptian reinforcements could reach Port Said from the south and unless it was quickly seized the defenders might well demolish it, preventing an advance southwards later on. With the French went a detachment of the British Guards Independent Parachute Company and a few Sappers from 9 Squadron. In charge of the latter was my 'P' course friend Graham Owens. I was to hear more of his doings later on.

One Frenchman was with us. François Collet had lived with the battalion for the past five days in our camp in Cyprus. As we made our preparations there, and the restless, infuriating wind drove dust into everything we packed and ate, he had won a special place in the hearts of all of us in the Officers' Mess. Imagine all that is best, all that you expect, in the quintessence of a Frenchman, and you have François. Urbane, gracious, humorous, modest, he charmed us all. He was attached to us so that he could call down French aircraft from the 'cab-rank' of ground-attack fighters which was to circle overhead in support of the landings. He was to work with our own Air Contact Team using the code-name *Robert*. Sartorially he did not fail our high hopes either. He was, to be accurate, a Commander in the French Navy, and on occasions wore a hat which would have done credit to a British Admiral. He was also a Commando and therefore had a green beret. Because he was attached to us he was issued with a maroon one. He would ring the changes on this collection of head-gear as seemed most appropriate at the time. He wore an imposing nautical beard and his uniform was decorated with the scarlet ribbon of the Legion d'Honneur on the left breast. Such a figure at large in the dusty, teeming spaces of Tunisia Camp was bound to attract attention.

We had seen the battalions of French *Paras* busying themselves round the outskirts of Nicosia during the last fortnight. Casual, sloppy figures they seemed, walking round in their rubber-soled boots and camouflaged loose-fitting olive and brown battle-suits. They looked after their own equipment and were often to be seen drying or packing their parachutes in a factory near the old city walls. These were not as infallibly packed as our X-type parachutes from Upper Heyford. François later took some of the battalion officers off for a jump with his compatriots. They emplaned in a Nord Atlas.

'Remember that, with us, this thing,' he said, significantly tapping his reserve parachute, 'is not an ornament.'

Casual and sloppy-looking or not, *les Paras* made us look a crowd of amateurs when it came to fighting experience. They had all soldiered for several years in Algeria, and before that many of them had survived the bitter debacle in Indo-China. François himself had been at Dien Bien Phu, where a desperate losing battle had been waged for weeks. Many of the French had not been home on leave for six years, which made our temporary absence from England seem pretty tame. François, as he jumped onto El Gamil airfield, was making his sixth jump into action, and about his two-hundredth in all.

I was making my ninth.

Down, twisting down obliquely, down the kaleidoscope of shapes and colours which surround you before the parachute opens. Turquoise sky, buff sand, slate sea and black smoke in a great pall towering out of the control tower buildings. The streaming, opening parachutes of the men ahead of me slanted across, below and behind against the sand. The white streaks of harness over their shoulders and the floss of the rigging-lines were light streaks against the darker distance. Twisting. Damn. Never get out of twists in 600 feet. The kaleidoscope whirled clockwise for one revolution and, with the sag of deceleration, whirled back again as the parachute opened. Relief. Without the reserve parachute I had felt more than ever a hostage to fortune on jumping. 'Look up!' Yes it's all there: wonderful thing. 'Look down!' How like the reconnaissance photographs, but in Technicolor, with fierce orange flames feeding that huge pillar of oily smoke.

'Look around!' No one near me in the air and no risk of entanglement with another parachutist. Rat-tat-tat from below and firing in all directions. Never heard so much shooting. We must be giving them hell. (In fact the first sticks had barely landed and all the shooting was *at* us.) Look down again. Little luminous glow-worms whizzing all over the view. Dully I never realised they were tracer bullets directed upwards from the ground.

The more experienced officers were not so ignorant. Ron Norman, who had himself opposed a parachute landing when the Germans invaded Crete, spent his time marking down the machine-gun posts round the airfield. He was so engrossed, as he floated to the ground, that he accidentally made a perfect 'stand-up' landing and had to lie down deliberately to take off his harness. Geoff Norton, commander of Support Company, watched the bullets arching up at him and suddenly found several of the rigging lines tumbling, severed around him. He had been lucky. Just before jumping Geoff had to clutch the doorway of his Hastings when an A.A. shell, bursting close by, made it slew on its side. The stick behind him staggered around in confusion and he had a moment's debate whether to jump or not. Then the red and green lights came on simultaneously and they had all tumbled out.

'Lower equipment!' The old Abingdon parrot-cries came back. Those hours spent on 'synthetic' in the big hangar were worthwhile after all. Pull out the release pin from the leg-strap. It *must* come free with all that butter on it. Getting this fouled had been one of my chief anxieties. Fine. Now just push the release hooks together and away it falls.

SMACK! A great whiplash in the right eye. Too hard to hurt at all. Not me, I thought. I can't have been hit. No, not me. The eye only registered white fog. I must have been hit. Then I must be dead. Whatever it was must have gone straight through my head and out the other side. At once I was in a flat off the Brompton Road. We were playing charades after dinner. Half a dozen medical students in their final year, playing 'Nelson's Eye'. One of us sat dressed as Horatio, an empty sleeve and half an orange held close to the face. Another was led in blindfold and introduced to the Lord.

'You remember how he lost his arm?' The empty sleeve was brought forward. 'And you remember the hat he used to wear.' The hat was duly fingered. 'And you remember how he lost an eye in battle?'

'Yes.'

'Well, there's the socket!' And the probing finger is thrust into the half orange. Screams of alarm.

My eye must feel just like that.

The equipment fell to the end of the nylon suspension cord, tweaked, and fell on free. I had lost it. Watch where it goes. That was the unpardonable sin, failing to attach your equipment properly. Sort that out later.

I raised my hand to the eye. No blood. No blood round the back of my neck either. That would be sorted out later too. So I was alive then. I mustn't make a mess of landing. I couldn't judge distance, and to sprain an ankle now would be really silly. I'd always been led to believe that the odds were in favour of coming through a battle unscathed. Here I was, winged in the first few seconds, and by Egyptians of all people.

But others were in worse plight. Gillespie, a private from 'C' Company, had just lowered his equipment in the air when he received a terrific blow in the groin. He felt for the damage and his hand returned wet with blood. One of the Sappers had his parachute canopy tattered by an A.A. shell and fell at alarming speed to the ground. He broke both legs on landing.

It was a sudden introduction to battle for the novices. In a matter of seconds we had been scattered like clay-pigeons for the defenders to practise on. Luckily for us incredulity remained the chief emotion as the sand approached.

'Feet and knees together.' Thump, crumble, crunch, forward to a light landing on damp sand. I rolled, and sand filled the release box which came undone with difficulty. Lopsidedly I struggled out of the harness and looked around for my equipment container which lay on the sand thirty yards away. In five hundred feet of descent I had only drifted that short distance. We had indeed been lucky with the wind. A stiff breeze would have dispersed us all over the edges of the airfield.

Even with perfect conditions the 'B' Company men who had jumped last were bound to land near the perimeter. Many of them came down within a few yards of the Egyptians defending the eastern edge of the airfield, and were in action at close range from the moment they hit the ground. Private Looker was involved straight away in hand-to-hand combat. As he neared the ground, just off the airfield, he watched an Egyptian shooting straight up at him from below. The Egyptian had climbed out of his slit trench to get a better view. A late oscillation of Looker's parachute swung his container like a giant pendulum which knocked the Egyptian sprawling into the trench. Looker landed a second later and in the ensuing scuffle came out on top.

So, from the beginning it was a case of kill or be killed. The boys who landed in Egypt that morning had no thought of the political aims or consequences of their actions. They had orders to capture the airfield. For months this was what their training had prepared them to do. If success entailed killing every Egyptian round the Dropping Zone they would do just that.

To start with the odds were against them. The defenders were dug in and had several machine-guns sited to cover the airfield. The only cover of any sort was provided by rows of empty 40-gallon oil-drums spread all over the sand. These were the 'Electric Mines' which some pessimist had spotted on the latest air photographs. Sergeant Sparvell of the Intelligence Section had been right.

Two men would have given anything to be back among the simple perils of the Dropping Zone. Both had jumped late and were far behind the Egyptian lines. Private Neal, a nursing orderly from the surgical team, had difficulty getting over the spar in the Valetta and when he jumped was well behind the rest of the stick. He landed in the sewage farm several hundred yards east of the airfield and made a long and desperate crawl back to our lines, under fire from both sides for much of the time. He brought his heavy and valuable load of surgical equipment all the way with him. Private Lamph of 'B' Company was in still worse plight. He fell down as he climbed over the spar and jumped eventually so late that the aircraft was heading north and just over the sea. As he came down he saw that he could direct his drift to land either in the sea or on the beach. He chose the sea and crashed into water, which proved to be waist-deep when he stood up. No sooner had he done so than a machine-gun opened up from the shore and a hail of bullets lashed the sea around him. He flopped down and feigned dead for a long time, until he could ease his rifle out of the container under water. Then he paddled his way by inches to the shore and 'feeling eight feet wide' dashed up the beach to take cover behind an oil drum. The situation demanded a smoke. But although his lighter worked, all his cigarettes were too sodden to ignite. He joined up with 'B' Company later in the day as they advanced towards Port Said.

At least Lamph had time in which to get his rifle out. His companions who landed at the edge of the airfield were under fire at once at close range. It took them thirty long seconds to get their weapons ready to shoot back. What they said later about the Sims weapon container cannot be printed. The Sten gun was described in similar language. It had been widely and successfully used in Europe during the war, but in sand it very quickly seized up. It was galling that many other units, even some policemen in Cyprus, were issued with the much more efficient Lanchester submachine-gun. In Egypt the parachutists cursed their stopped guns, threw them away and replaced them with the much better Birettas, Schmeissers or Russian Carbines with which their enemies were armed. Everyone felt that a little more government expenditure on transport aircraft and good infantry weapons would have made their jobs a lot easier.

I thought with anxiety and thanks of the 'B' Company boys as I ran over to collect my container. They were between me and the enemy. Hell was let loose all over the airfield as far as I could make out with my one working eye. The rattle of small arms fire was continuous round the eastern edge. The whip-like cracks near me were puzzling. Then I remembered my father saying that bullets passing close by made this noise. He had been an M.O. on the Somme and should know. I lay down in the sand behind the container. It formed a very penetrable shield, between me and the bullets. I undid the clumsy buckles, opened the flaps and pulled the 'quick release' string.

The 'quick release' was made by lashing the equipment into the container with a sort of blanket-stitch, running in loops, between two sets of eyelets. In theory you pulled the end of the string and it all came undone. I pulled. It jammed. Machine-gun bullets came splattering across the sand towards me twenty yards away. Bloody thing! Gippo bastards! I suppose Celtic ancestry will show up at times like this. I became insensately, blindly furious. Of course the Egyptians didn't recognise the Red Cross on my sleeve (poor devils, they couldn't even see it). They had hit me once, and looked like doing so again. I pulled out my 9 mm. automatic and discharged it four or five times in the direction of the enemy thinking 'That'll make the so-and-so's keep their heads down.' This relieved my feelings a lot.

Then, more logically, I found a penknife and cut the beastly string, and retrieved my battered, perforated Bergen rucksack. It had fallen free for five hundred feet and was badly distorted. A small hole penetrated the bottom and there was a larger one in the flap at the top. The suspension cord of the container was severed and molten at the end. Whatever did the damage must have been red hot. That at least was satisfactory. It had fallen free through enemy action, not my own incompetence.

I sat on the ground and elbowed my way into the straps. The thing was too heavy to lift onto my back. I looked up at the sky where the Hastings, flying in pairs were coming in to drop their loads. At the west end of the airfield the 'Heavy Drops' plumetted away, and their great quadruple white parachutes burst like white plumes against the blue beyond. They flew on, and the sticks of parachutists spewed out. Flashes and black puffs of smoke splashed among them. More or less accurate A.A. fire. That must have been what hit me. I lumbered to my feet and jogged off westwards towards the control tower buildings.

Behind my back as I went were 'B' Company, battling at close quarters with the Egyptians. For what seemed an age to each of them they could only unpack and be shot at. Two enemy machine guns in pits, and riflemen shooting at them from a few houses near the north east corner of the airfield, made it an ugly moment. They were lucky that there were no Russians in the Egyptian positions. A little more experience and determination on the part of the defenders would have prevented many of them ever leaving those empty, unprotected few acres of sand. Some of the boys were hit and two killed as they returned the fire, lying there in the open. One of them was mortally wounded as he landed among the Egyptian slit trenches. Within seconds of landing the company had lost between five and ten per cent of its strength. Mortar bombs began to fall and unless they moved quickly the losses would increase.

Dick Stevens, the Company Commander, could see it all. Most of his men lacked the experience to realise the need for speed. Shouting like a madman he rallied a bunch of men together and they cleared the houses of enemy. As he charged in towards the buildings a mortar splinter 'quite a slow moving thing, I saw it coming', sliced into the ball of his thumb. Karl Beale his second-in-command dressed the wound for him and gave him an injection of morphia. After which, according to Karl, he went off as happy as a sandboy.

131

I had my back to all this and staggered, in fits and starts, towards the control tower. A series of sharp cracks close to my head made me flop down behind an oil drum. Behind the next one, a few yards away, was the familiar figure of Corporal Dunbavin. Stray bullets cracked and spattered around us. The corporal was furious.

"Who's got a rifle?" he called over his shoulder. The riflemen nearby were intent on reaching their own Company areas. One paused for a moment.

"Get that bastard with the Bren gun over there!" called the Corporal pointing at a tiny figure at the southern edge of the airfield. The head and gun popped up for a few seconds and a burst of fire sprayed the area around us. The rifleman crouched beside us, decided that the target was not worth the effort, and moved on. The corporal told him what he thought about this, very clearly.

'Could you take a look at my eye?' The corporal kindly crawled over and took a look.

'Swollen, but doesn't look too bad.'

'We'd better go on then.'

We lurched to our feet and headed for the control tower once more. After a few yards our running degenerated into jogging and then we frankly walked. Looking around, it was just like Frensham Common all over again. Innumerable figures were strolling across the scene. Each was carrying too much weight to move any faster. Bullets were cracking all over the place, mortar bombs began to fall to our right, and from time to time great balls of fire tore along the length of the runway overhead. These were missiles fired by a rocket projector somewhere on the outskirts of Port Said. Amid all this the Toms ambled about their appointed tasks.

'I thought "These Englishmen, they are either very brave, or very stupid",' said François afterwards. "Then I saw the face of one of them, and I knew.'

But in fact they could not do otherwise. With their enormous loads, running was impossible for more than a few yards at a time. They could only leave their vital equipment and run, or carry it and walk. There was, however, no need to spring to one's feet and take photographs, which was what Private Castelnuovo did on landing.

He was batman to Noel Hodgson. A small, compact man, with bushy black hair and startling eyebrows. Quiet, well-spoken, you would guess the perfect gentleman's gentleman. He was also a fanatical amateur photographer. As soon as he could get out of his harness he was on one knee, snapping a couple of quick shots as a Hastings disgorged its passengers above him. Then a rapid panorama of views round the Dropping Zone. Noel found the first few minutes on landing reminded him unpleasantly of battles in Korea, and had to point out to Castelnuovo that the enemy were not firing blanks.

The wandering figures made for the destinations which each of them knew by heart. The control tower buildings and a prominent iron tower at the east end of the airfield made it fairly easy to orientate oneself. Many of us, Battalion Headquarters, and the recently formed 'D' Company which Noel Hodgson commanded, were heading for the control tower. Our anaesthetist Malcolm Elliott walked briskly towards a tower and only discovered from the nearness of the 'B' Company battle that it was the wrong one. Norman Kirby, the surgeon, was making his way westwards with an orderly of the Field Ambulance when a mortar bomb landed just between them. It was a dud, but Norman still swears he can taste the sand which filled his mouth as he dived to escape it.

The corporal and I walked on. There was Horace with a huge grin, pulling the walking stick out of his container. A burning container lay in our path. What a pity not to salvage it, I thought, as we walked close by. It contained mortar bombs and went up with a mighty roar a short time later.

'A' Company had cleared the buildings by the time we reached them. This had been fairly straightforward, as opposition was slight. But one member of the company had the disconcerting experience of viewing his companions attack through enemy eyes. Private Pugsley was dropped so that his parachute became entangled in one of the tall palm trees just outside the control tower. As the attack on the buildings was pressed home Pugsley, suspended a few feet above the ground, found British bullets smacking past him into the control tower. Mike Walsh who was directing the attack has a vivid memory of the outraged, incredulous figure swinging in his harness saying, 'Cor—me. Cor—me' repeatedly as they swept past.

We rounded the corner, and there was our Company Commander, Lawrence, positively genial he seemed.

'R.A.P. in the garage at the back over there doc. What's happened to your eye?'

'Some bastard shot me with an anti-aircraft gun.'

'Holden, show the medical officer to his position.'

And there, unmoved as ever, was my batman Holden. His large, fair face crumpled into a grin as we met. We went round to the garage with our weapons at the ready and broke in through a side door, coming face to face with the Company Sergeant Major, breaking out. Luckily no one fired.

Inside the garage we met up with Norman Kirby, showing no traces of his meal of sand, and Malcolm Elliott, who had walked back from the 'B' Company area secure in the knowledge that his anaesthetic machine, on his back, lay between him and the enemy. So by ones and twos the Advanced Dressing Station staff assembled. To start with we were to work together, the Regimental Aid Post staff—myself, sergeant, corporal and orderlies—would be under one roof with the Surgical Team and section of the Field Ambulance. Later on we would probably act independently, sending casualties back to the Advanced Dressing Station.

A medical orderly was attached to each Company. First Aid to the wounded would be given initially by the man's companions, then by the Company medical orderly. He would be evacuated back to the Regimental Aid Post, from where he would pass to the Surgical Team if sufficiently urgent, or be held in the Advanced Dressing Station if his wounds were not desperately serious. Then . . . God only knew what would happen then. Our plans could allow for a good deal of uncertainty and variation, but the whole Operation being put forward a day was not among the contingencies which we, or the Medical authorities above us, had foreseen. We knew that on November 6th evacuation of casualties by helicopter was to be laid on. Today was November 5th. Whether our resources were able to tide us over till tomorrow depended on the number of casualties.

Unobtrusively, as only those who really know what they are doing can, Norman took charge. 'Theatre in here,' he said, as we looked into an office at the near end of the garage. 'Preparation and sterilising in the workshop at the back. And there'll be plenty of room for Reception and Treatment in the main garage.'

The main garage was a building about fifteen yards long and open at the south side. The roof and walls seemed solid enough.

'We'd better get rid of all this glass,' said Norman. 'We don't want it flying about later on.' And for a few happy minutes we broke every window in the place, knocking the panes clear with our weapons. The Theatre was ready, architecturally, for whatever might arrive.

We did not have to wait long. The first casualties came in within minutes. Parachute accidents to start with. Peter Woods of the *Daily Mirror*, with badly jarred ankles—all his tales of previous parachuting experience were just eyewash! Then the Sapper with broken legs, and one of the boys who had hit the control tower on landing, suffering from severe bruises.

The Colonel was not among them, so he must have missed the runway, despite his prophecy to the contrary at our briefing.

As 'B' Company collected their wounded and reloaded their weapons after clearing the houses, the mortaring continued. In a brief spell of action the company had lost heavily. They had fulfilled their first task, but counting the cost was a sorry business. The wounded were treated and sent back to the control tower.

Two figures in berets appeared among them, walking with unconcern through the mortar bombs and stray small arms fire. It was Colonel Crook and Brigadier Butler. The effect of this visit on the company was electric.

CHAPTER VIII

SAND, SEWAGE AND CEMETERY

To the Colonel's and Brigadier's behaviour, the snide rejoinder would be 'heroics'. In fact they had simply gone forward to see how the company leading the advance towards Port Said was getting on. No amount of wireless reports could replace knowledge gained at first hand. The Brigadier had joined the Battalion Group in the assault almost as an afterthought. The airborne operation was initially to involve two battalions only—ourselves and the French. But when the operation was put forward to November 5th it was felt that an overall commander should accompany us to handle any political or strategic decisions on the spot, and somewhat naturally the appointment had fallen to Tubby. Knowing him, we would suspect that his own machinations also had something to do with it. Effectively, he was at present a mere observer. He had deputed the job of capturing the airfield to 3 PARA, and in the same way Colonel Crook had deputed the clearing of the east end to 'B' Company. This was Dick Stevens's battle but if he needed support the Colonel would see that he got it.

It would not have occurred to either of them to take cover from the mortaring and scattered small arms fire. Though Tubby did go so far as to administer a severe ticking off to Jim Burke, the Intelligence officer, who unthinkingly walked up and saluted him in full view of the enemy. Compliments to officers are waived in the front lines, and this was inviting special attention by snipers. But the job of getting forward brooked no delay and both of them had experienced much worse than this in other, fiercer battles.

To analyse the final deciding motive one must look at it from the other end of the telescope. The private soldier's end.

137

You are nineteen. Two years ago you were still at school, in the outskirts of Wolverhampton. Then along comes this National Service. You think 'Damn peeling spuds for two years. I'll have a go at the Paras.' And you have a go. You survive 'P' course, Abingdon and a few months of Cyprus. Smashing really. And then these Gippos. All laid on. A piece of cake. Air support, anti-tank guns, the lot. Done a dozen jumps already, what if this is the thirteenth? And we come down just like they said. Right place and all. But Christ! The shooting! One mate dead and three wounded in minutes. Follow the Platoon commander off the D.Z. Christ! Keep down and yer tin hat on. Then blimey! If it's not the C.O. and Brigadier wandering around in berets. If they can get away with it, so can I.

This, or something like it, must have gone on in many of the minds which were still reeling under the sudden impacts of killing for the first time and of watching friends, like animals, instantly blotted out or maimed. Subconsciously perhaps the two officers knew the effect their promenade would have on the boys who were doing the fighting. For, whatever their faults as soldiers, Paul Crook and Tubby Butler knew their men. They knew how recently some of them had joined the brigade. And they were not themselves old enough to have forgotten what it was like to be under fire for the first time.

'B' Company had distinguished themselves already. After this they never looked back.

At the opposite, western end of the airfield it was not quiet. After clearing the control tower buildings 'A' Company went on to attack a pill-box containing a medium machine gun which was sweeping the Dropping Zone. The task of wiping out this strongpoint was given by Mike Walsh to 1 platoon, commanded by Peter Coates. The subalterns of the battalion were all young, keen, adventurous and all too prone to get into minor mischief, just as their forerunners in 1944 had been. Peter stood out among them as being just a little wilder than the rest. He was slender, fair haired and with a fanatical glint in his eye. When a plot was brewing, he could usually be depended on to go one further than anyone else. It is just possible though that the job he was given caused the glint to fade momentarily. The platoon of thirty men had to attack a well-constructed pill-box four hundred yards away across flat sand, in the face of constant machine gun fire.

They moved in a series of bounds, using slight undulations in the sand as stopping points. One section of ten men gave covering fire while the others moved. The first bound took them without loss to the first ridge of sand, two hundred yards from the pill-box. The second one to within a hundred yards of it.

Mike Walsh could only watch. He had taught them how to do this attack. They had practised it again and again in Cyprus and the movements were second nature to them. But in Cyprus there had been no opposition. Now, as he saw his young soldiers going through the drill they had rehearsed, faultlessly, and without a thought for themselves in the hail of bullets, Mike found himself swallowing hard.

Lying down, pressed into the slender shelter of that last ripple in the sand, Peter saw that he would lose men if they went on further like this. At closer range the Egyptians were bound to hit some of them.

'Clements!' he called. And a small stocky man came up, carrying a 3·5 inch rocket launcher. Clements had a level stare beneath his unlined brow and curly hair. A cool customer. Peter explained what was needed. Clements nodded assent. He crouched in position and his Number 2 loaded the bomb and set the firing mechanism. Acting as Number 2 on the rocket launcher requires some skill. If you are careless it is easy to get your head blown off when the rocket is fired, and close teamwork is vital. They managed it all perfectly, despite the enemy fire.

Clements aimed and fired. The bomb bounced short and whizzed over the top of the pillbox. They reloaded, kneeling in full view of the machine gun facing them. The second bomb either went through the aperture or burst just beside it. The machine gun fire stopped and Peter led his men forward. They overran the pillbox, killing two of the defenders and taking nine prisoners.

True to form, Peter was in trouble shortly after this success. Acting on his own initiative, he sent a party of men off to search for ammunition to use in a captured enemy machine gun. Mike Walsh, his company commander, thought this patrol a dangerous and unnecessary one and told him so, very definitely.

Between 'A' and 'B' Companies, battling at either end of the airfield, there was a large expanse of sand and runways, dotted with empty oil drums. On this half-square-mile of Egypt the remainder of the battalion was diversely but fully occupied. 'C' Company were to clear the south side of the Dropping Zone and then concentrate as reserve company for the attack eastwards towards Port Said itself. During this phase Philip Butterworth distinguished himself as a marksman. Philip was the quietest subaltern in the Officers' Mess at that time: a shy smile would illuminate his face briefly when things became wild, but I had the feeling that a lot of the slapstick comedy which went on left him cold. While the airfield was still being saturated with parachutists from the sky Philip found himself under machine gun fire at a range of two hundred yards. He lay down the instant he spotted the enemy gun, adjusted his sights as though he were on the range, and shot the Egyptian Bren-gunner dead.

For Headquarters and 'D' Companies their work really began once the airfield was captured. These companies provided the parties who were to 'de-crate' the jeeps which had been dropped with us. Unless the jeeps could rapidly be loaded with their anti-tank guns and driven to their appointed positions there was a very real possibility that tanks could swarm up to the airfield perimeter and wreak havoc on the lightly-armed parachutists. The 'de-crating' parties had a bad time. Through the desultory mortar fire they made for the vehicles which sat on their metal crash-pans at the western end of the airfield. The Russian rockets roared, like comets, close overhead. They reached the jeeps and unshackled the huge white parachutes. It was simply a question of pushing the jeeps so that the wheels rolled out of the crash-pans. These should have been flattened by the impact as the load hit the ground. But in that soft sand the pans were intact. They pushed, cursed, tugged and rocked, while bullets cracked past and the mortar bombs threw up clouds of sand. Eventually most of the jeeps were freed and driven over to pick up their '106' anti-tank guns and ammunition. The sweating, panting groups of soldiers went on with the work of collecting containers into a supply area, under the vigilant eye of Chippy Robinson. He had accompanied the airborne assault while Bob Grainger the Quartermaster supervised supplies with the 'sea tail' following behind us.

The British War Machine was rusty, that was the unpalatable truth. Lack of recent fighting experience had projected the battalion into action from inadequate transport aircraft, with obsolete heavy-drop equipment, with a cumbersome and impractical personal weapon container, and with second-rate personal weapons. Graham Owens, who accompanied the French onto the 'sporting D.Z.' near the Ferdan bridge, found a sorry contrast between their equipment and his own. Through recent bitter tribulations the French had learnt how to make the machine work smoothly and how to survive in an opposed landing such as this one. Flying into heavy anti-aircraft fire at 450 feet the French pilots dropped their battalion with great accuracy onto the narrow strip of sand. No one fell in the water.

Graham came down near the edge of the Dropping Zone, and was immediately fired on at close range by several Egyptians. For what seemed an eternity of seconds he could only lie in a nearby ditch struggling to get his Sten gun out of his Sims container. To rub the point home a Frenchman landed in the telephone wires alongside him, dropped lithely to the ground with his light pack and carbine, and was shooting back before Graham was armed ready to emerge into the battle.

The French were tough. They and the British Guardsmen with them endured ten minutes of gruelling machine gunning and mortar fire, as the defenders of the bridge tried to wipe them out. Then, as soon as radio contact was made with the Corsairs and Thunderstreaks circling overhead, they prepared to move. The aircraft dived to strafe the bridge, and they charged beneath the blanket of cannon shells and machine-gun fire above them. It was over in a matter of minutes. The bridge was taken.

Graham examined the piles of the bridge. It was not mined. The defenders had not had the chance to place the charges in position and they were found in a hut some distance away.

For his part in this action Graham was subsequently mentioned in despatches. I met him a fortnight after it occurred. Characteristically he made little of his own efforts. But I could guess that they had been considerable. He was unchanged yet different. His face was as fresh and open as before, and the dark eyes were lit by the same curiosity and interest. But instead of the tough, amiable schoolboy who had shared my room on 'P' course, here was someone older. A contemporary, or senior to myself. It was as if ten varied, ageing years of life had been compressed into the same number of minutes, there in the sand and mud by the Ferdan bridge.

Tough as he was, our own Frenchman François admitted that he was impressed by the cold-blooded way in which Peter Coates's platoon had dealt with the pillbox at the edge of the airfield. François was anxious to get his wireless working as soon as possible and set to work to assemble his aerial on the roof of one of the buildings. As he was doing so a Russian *S.U. 100* self-propelled gun on the edge of Port Said found the range of the control tower and hammered several armour-piercing shells through it. Without hurrying or checking François completed his preparations.

'*Ici Robert.*' And he was on the air. It became a catchword throughout the battalion for weeks afterwards.

Paradoxically it was the nonchalance of the British Toms which struck him most.

'You are an impossible people! Look at these men. They *walk* off the Dropping Zone under fire, stroll around as if in barracks, and the only excitement I've seen was when somebody shouted "Anybody for char?" Then they all ran!'

Nonchalance for François reached a climax later on. He had been brought up, with all *les Paras*, to maintain his own equipment and treat parachutes with due respect. Imagine, then, his horror, on rounding a corner, to find one of the boys solemnly sawing up a parachute with a jack knife, to line his slit trench with it.

'My man, you know how much a parachute costs?'

'Yes, sir,' not looking up but sawing methodically on. 'Ninety pounds, sir.'

The luxury of slit trenches of any sort, let alone silk-lined ones, was not one that 'B' Company could yet afford. They were to advance eastwards towards Port Said. Initially they had to cross a patch of broken ground before entering the reed-beds of the sewage farm beyond. As they did so the first of their casualties were brought in to us.

And they were bad ones. The jeeps which took the anti-tank guns forward to their positions alongside the road had come straight back with the more serious cases. It is hard to imagine the damage which high-velocity missiles inflict on living tissues. Having once seen it, you do not forget.

But it was bewildering: there were a penetrating chest wound, several compound fractures, a shattered knee joint, an innocent-looking little wound above the elbow. Above it the arm was ominously swollen. His right arm. I felt for the pulse at the wrist. Absent. The artery was divided and the arm would die.

'Not my arm, sir? Not my arm!'

'Don't worry. We'll get it right.'

We didn't, and nor did anyone else.

I brought Norman through from his preparations. They were having trouble with the Primus stoves and boiling up instruments was taking time. Nevertheless it was important to decide an order of priorities. We arranged the first few cases for operation near the 'Theatre' and went back to check the new arrivals.

Within a short time the place was half full.

This was the cost of Police Action. Yesterday they had all been fit, strong, tough, invincible. Now they were white-faced with shock, quiet, bleeding, dying. The battalion was paying for its efforts. Getting maudlin about it was unlikely to help. I wished to God that I even felt the action was right.

SLAM! SLAM! SLAM! The shells burst closer and closer outside. Feeling a rotten coward, I flopped into the empty inspection pit in the garage. If the roof came in, the wounded lying on their stretchers hadn't got a hope. After six explosions the shelling stopped and I clambered sheepishly out again. The orderlies had flattened themselves instinctively. Only pock marks in the wall remained. Jim Burke had returned from the 'B' Company area and was just outside during this bombardment. He flung himself into the nearest slit trench, only to find that he had been preceded by two soldiers with reactions rather faster than his own. As the splinters hissed over him he felt hopelessly exposed, and he had to endure vociferous complaints from the lower depths of the trench.

Norman Morley, the mortar officer ducked at the first shell, and received a terrific blow on the head which dazed him. He was brought in to us with a large triangular gash in his steel helmet, and a very small one in the scalp beneath it. After the surgical team had dealt with his wound he sat about for some time recovering, and then insisted on returning to duty.

This was tame compared with the steady toll exacted by mortar fire on 'B' Company as they advanced.

Dick Stevens had been standing with the Colonel, discussing the next moves. Karl Beale, his second-in-command, had just moved away to one side when there was the crash of a close detonation. A shout. Karl looked round and there was Dick on the ground, his leg shattered below the knee. Karl gave him a second shot of morphia and he was evacuated by jeep.

Karl turned to the more pressing duty of commanding 'B' Company.

Responsibility came lightly to Karl. A short man with steady grey eyes and dark hair, he gave an impression of unhurried thoughtfulness at all times. The immense fumes of his curly-stemmed pipe usually enhanced his appearance. Just now the pipe was unlit. Karl chewed the stem as he briefed his platoon commanders.

The company moved on. Once they were into the reeds of the sewage farm, two platoons went forward on either flank, and one remained slightly behind in the centre. On the left flank the platoon was commanded by 'Pompey' Norman. The company was a subaltern short, leaving Sergeant Norman to take charge of one of the platoons. In a battalion containing many vivid characters none was more widely known than Pompey. His nickname derived from his home town Portsmouth. He spoke with the soft, full vowels that they use in Hampshire. No one, meeting him out of uniform, would have thought that the short, bulky man, with a young, almost cherubic face, was one of the toughest sergeants in 3 PARA. His bulkiness was entirely due to muscle, and by weight lifting, basket ball and Rugby football he kept it extremely fit. Pompey could lead a platoon, not through force or bombast, but simply by doing everything better and for longer than his men. They would naturally imitate him, and automatically obey his orders, for he was considerate and kindly. It would not occur to anyone to cross Pompey unnecessarily. He took a section of ten men with him and set off along the road, between the reeds of the sewage farm and the beach on the left. Five hundred yards down the road towards Port Said was a pillbox from which fire was directed at them. They halted some distance short of it while mortar support was laid on.

As they lay there, waiting for the bombs to plaster the target, it seemed a long time. To move nearer the pillbox was certain to invite casualties. Enough wounded had gone back to the dressing station already. Enough lay dead.

The first bomb was a 'short', and splattered them with sand and splinters. Pompey had a few strong words about this later on with the mortar sergeant. It was no fault of his. This is one of the inevitable hazards of the 3-inch mortar. In Norman Morley's absence the mortar sergeant handled his platoon with great skill. Most of the precious six hundred-odd bombs which had come with the first air-lift landed on their targets.

The bombardment of the pillbox was brief but cruel. The vicious splashing bursts surrounded it in a mantle of dust, illuminated only by the hollow, clanging, orange flashes as more bombs exploded. It stopped, and in the pause, which seemed almost silent, Pompey and his men stormed forward. Several Egyptians were killed.

As this attack went on the anti-tank gunners kept watch. Bill Hill, the Lieutenant commanding the anti-tank platoon had come forward with two guns. He wanted to make sure that whatever problems arose, tanks would not be one of them. They spotted a dug-in tank down the road, firing on the 'B' Company soldiers as they advanced. One round from the '106' silenced it. When the wreckage was overrun later it turned out to have been only an anti-tank gun. But the '106' had proved itself. A short time afterwards the anti-tank gunners blasted a building which the enemy were using as an observation post.

On the right flank of the 'B' Company front the advance through thick reeds was not easy. There were many Egyptian snipers concealed in the dense cover, and winkling them out was a harrowing business. Chris Hogg was in command of the platoon involved. He was a serious-minded subaltern aged nineteen, who took the complex task of managing his platoon in deadly earnest. He had reason to. Through no fault of his, they had had more than their fair share of disasters in the Cyprus days. Now it was a more straightforward problem. More frightening perhaps, but simpler. They were to advance to the forward end of the sewage farm, beyond some buildings at its right-hand or southern edge. When contact was made with the enemy they were to report back to Karl Beale.

Beyond the thick reeds was an open area where sewage was treated in concrete troughs. This was quickly crossed, and they ran for the buildings which were unoccupied. Here they made ready for the next bound forward. After some rough ground and rubbish tips a great rolling expanse of sand dunes led eastwards to the wall of the cemetery three hundred yards away.

They formed up in open order and advanced out of the rubbish tips. Intense fire greeted them from the direction of the cemetery wall.

There was nothing to do except go to ground. Chris and his men dropped behind a low bank. Bullets smacked and clattered among the empty tins and bottles which littered it.

Contact with the enemy had been made. They must return.

Round the buildings they crawled or ran and back towards the open concrete troughs. The Egyptian fire now was sporadic and the buildings shielded them from it.

But in the open ground they were spotted by two French Mystéres, which mistook them for Egyptians.

At the first strafing they dived gratefully into the sewage-filled troughs. There was a dried crust on top of the stinking slush underneath which was just strong enough to bear their weight. They could only cringe helplessly against the concrete walls as the storm of cannon shells and machine gun bullets swept over them. One aircraft came round again and again and then the second one joined in.

That was enough. Incredibly no one had yet been hit. But if this went on they would all become casualties sooner or later. Chris told them to run for it, back to the cover of the thick reeds behind them. It was the fastest hundred yards they had ever done.

Breathless, foul-smelling and covered in sweat, they all returned. Chris Hogg reported what had happened to Karl Beale. Ron Norman was standing by as he did so. 'C'

Company was to take over for the next attack and Ron had come forward to arrange the details of the move forward. For Ron it roused many memories. The grimy, sewage bespattered young man standing there giving his careful report. The fear, excitement, despair and relief of the last few minutes animated his face as he did so. Fifteen years ago, not so very far away, in Crete, Ron had given the same sort of reports himself during the German invasion of the Island. He found himself sympathising with Chris as the forgotten experience rose, like a Phoenix, from the ashes of memory.

Fortune had been kind. The platoon had been lucky to get through to the buildings without loss. Luckier still to survive the mistaken attack by the French aircraft.

The attack was an unfortunate exception and no blame for it attached to François or the Air Contact Team. The two French pilots were acting without orders, and had simply not thought that our troops could be so far forward within a short time of landing. The regular ground support aircraft had been otherwise faultless and very accurate. Within fifteen minutes of the drop it had been possible to call down air strikes on selected targets, and these had saved time and lives as the 'B' Company advance pressed forward. As the day wore on it became an accepted routine that whenever the troops were held up by Egyptian defensive positions an air strike was called down to pulverise them.

So dawn became morning, and with the heat of the sun came the flies. We had seen nothing like the clouds of them which swarmed round the Dressing Station. There was plenty to attract them. Blood-soaked dressings lay in profusion everywhere.

Holden, my batman, reacted characteristically to this state of affairs.

'Shall I dig a pit to put all this muck in, sir?'

And he dug an immense hole just outside the door, big enough to last for several days at our present rate of progress. Into it I had to throw most of the contents of my rucksack.

The tin of self-heating soup had exploded inside it. Several bottles of Dextran, which had been included for transfusion to casualties, were so much powdered glass. The canvas roll full of instruments had survived the fall, but the instruments themselves were all slightly warped. Luckily at the moment they were not needed, for Norman Kirby's equipment was doing most of the work.

As soon as their preparations were complete the surgical team had begun to operate on a severe chest wound. Three of the medical orderlies, including the anaesthetist's batman, gave a pint of blood to help resuscitate the wounded man. It was during this operation that Gerald Mullins, the Adjutant, inadvertently walked into the operating theatre. Major surgery is a gory affair to the uninitiated and Gerald quickly walked out again. He had begun the day on a ghoulish note by landing near Jim Burke the Intelligence Officer, Gerald found Jim doubled up over his container, groaning. With the sounds of battle at close quarters Gerald naturally assumed that Jim had been hit. In fact, being a bad air traveller, he was just being heartily sick.

Closing the chest wound was the first of six major operations they performed that day. In between cases they helped with our work in the main garage.

'Becoming a bit crowded in here,' said Norman, gently wiping a few spots of blood from his spectacles. 'We'd better try to lay on some evacuation.'

He went off to find Gerald again and put in a request for helicopter evacuation, to be relayed to the Navy offshore. This had already been arranged by the prompt action of the Brigade Major. We went back to the wounded in the garage. Anywhere would be better than where they lay now in the heat and buzzing flies, with the risk of further shelling at any moment. Our small supply of stretchers was running low, and we could do with more dressings and more water.

It was not a long wait. Half an hour later in a great swirling cloud of dust a Naval helicopter landed thirty yards away from the garage. The pilot was clearly anxious not to lose his machine by enemy action on the ground, for he kept his rotors spinning. He also wore his 'bone dome' helmet, and what with this covering his ears, the rotor blades swishing overhead, and the roar of the motor, conversation was virtually impossible. Very quickly he threw out a pile of stretchers and some water cans and by shouting and signs indicated that he could take two stretcher cases and three sitting.

Sergeant Rabet took me over the casualties and we decided who should be flown out first. The sergeant had been out of sight for some time. As soon as we had taken the garage over he had devoted a lot of energy to its sole occupant. At that stage this was an ancient truck with flat tyres. A good deal of tinkering had been necessary before he had proudly disappeared in a blare of noise and clouds of black smoke, driving on the rims. He had just returned from the 'B' Company area, grinning broadly. The lorry was full of holes—and casualties. The tyres by now were in shreds. But for the rest of that day the old truck did great service as our ambulance. The few jeeps worked hard too, but the carriage of ammunition and stores was their primary business.

It may have been on this old truck that Horace plied to and fro. From time to time he had appeared in the Dressing Station but from several of the wounded we heard that he had also helped in despatching them from their company areas at the edge of the airfield. The tough, ordinary, irreligious young men had found a lot of comfort in the Padre's presence, as the shadow of death passed near them.

We sorted out five of them who seemed closest to the shadow, and the orderlies carried and helped them to the helicopter. Loading them on board was a fiddling performance with straps and buckles. Then in a swirling dust storm they were off.

Dick Stevens arrived at the garage as we returned. Despite Karl Beale's double dose of morphia he was in a lot of pain and his face wore the grey, drawn expression of a man severely shocked. Gently the orderlies fixed a Thomas splint on his leg and re-dressed the ragged gash in his hand. Hard bitten as they were, the orderlies could be very gentle when they tried.

From Dick, and the boys who were brought in with him, we learned a little of what had happened in their battle, and what was going to come next.

This was to be an attack by 'C' Company on the Egyptian position in the cemetery. The company would have to form up at the forward edge of the sewage farm, ready to cross the expanse of sand towards the near wall of the cemetery. It was from positions behind this wall that the Egyptians had directed such heavy fire at Chris Hogg and his platoon. The cemetery lay beyond. It stretched for about six hundred yards, a mass of graves of all denominations. The innumerable headstones and tombs made a strong defensive position.

If 'C' Company were not to lose heavily the position would have to be softened up a good deal.

Ron Norman held an 'O' Group with his second-in-command and platoon commanders. They had moved forward through the 'B' Company lines, and the Egyptian mortar fire had caused several casualties among them as they did so. The company was in a suppressed, angry mood. But their turn to do something about it was coming. Meanwhile they dug in.

With their shovels it did not take long to get under cover. Private Penning had lost his shovel somewhere along the journey, but more than held his own in the race to get below ground, using an Airborne mug. He was a sandy haired reservist from Enfield. He would probably shudder to hear himself described as a cockney, but he shared the cockney gift of being able to describe the most terrifying, sad or moving experiences so that the overall effect is hilariously funny. He was in the platoon commanded by Jack Richardson, forming part of the 'thin red line' which was to attack the cemetery wall. Jack had a streak of fanaticism about him. Short cropped dark hair above a broad forehead and steely grey eyes which penetrated everything. A dedicated Roman Catholic,

151

his faith contributed a large share towards his apparently nerve-less form of courage. Of such stuff the early martyrs were made. He knew his men well. Knew that Penning had only married a week before the battalion returned to Cyprus from England in the summer. He could probably guess at the pangs of home-sickness which the young reservist had endured on the flight that morning.

Now for Penning it was simply a matter of following 'Mr. Richardson' into the cemetery, no matter what happened first.

They were to attack at 1030, after a mortar bombardment and air strike on the cemetery wall at 1028. On the carefully synchronised watches the dying seconds ticked away. Exactly on time the whine of the diving aircraft came overhead as the Venoms and Sea Hawks of the Fleet Air Arm plummetted down. From a huge height they steadied themselves exactly on their slender target and dived on. Only a few hundred feet above the ground the rockets blasted away from beneath their wings, to smash into towering explosions on the wall. The planes soared lightly upwards to prepare for the next dive.

The Egyptian position was shattered.

A few well-aimed rounds from the '106' near the road com-pleted the destruction. The medium machine guns on the south flank began to hammer spitefully at anything that still moved.

And at precisely 1030 the thin red line surged forward.

Watching them go, Ron was struck by the steadiness of his young soldiers in their first battle. Like Mike Walsh earlier in the day he thought how like an exercise it all looked. The troops advanced in open order, regardless of enemy fire, towards their first objective three hundred yards away across the rolling, low sand dunes. After a few minutes, without encountering serious opposition, they reached the cemetery wall.

It was a shambles. A fitting tribute to the accuracy of the air strike. Weapons and equipment were everywhere, and numerous dead Egyptians. Penning was amazed at the count-less pairs of boots, more than he had ever seen at one time without feet in them. He reckoned their owners could run quicker barefoot.

They pushed on through the cemetery. Clearing the enemy out of the enormous graveyard was rather like a lethal form of the surprise arcade in a fun fair. Sudden bursts of fire would come from behind tombs, or unexpected hollows in the ground. The morning passed slowly as they battled cautiously forward. They were not exactly trigger-happy, but it was a case of kill or be killed, and they took very few chances. And fewer prisoners.

Rounding the corner of one of the larger tombs Private Beech was about to open fire with his Bren gun to cover his comrades' advance. A sudden noise behind made him turn.

A few yards away an Egyptian had him covered with a rocket launcher. The firing mechanism had failed.

Beech took aim quickly and fired a burst.

The Colonel was watching this bloody engagement from the roof of one of the sewage farm buildings, which gave him a grandstand view of the 'C' Company attack. Geoff Norton the Support Company commander visited him during the morning and was glad to come down later from this exposed viewpoint. It seemed to draw a lot of enemy fire, to which the Colonel seemed oblivious.

At the far end of the cemetery the 'C' Company soldiers watched angrily as many of their enemies escaped southwards down the Manzala canal, in felluccas and any small boats they could find. Intermingled with them were numerous civilians. Ron Norman had a sharp argument with his rather blood-thirsty men about the pros and cons of opening fire. It was decreed they should not.

And so they diced along the razor edge which divides an act of war from an atrocity. Some of us, non-combatants, may have thought that the whole operation was morally wrong, and constituted an atrocity in itself. But none of the soldiers could indulge in this point of view. To do so would render them incapable of doing their job. As they squeezed their triggers and threw their grenades, they could not admit that what they were doing was wrong. Nor was it. They were simply carrying out their orders. '*Befehl ist Befehl.*'

Eichmann and the Auschwitz guards had made the same defence when they were called to account for their crimes. But there is a difference between winning a battle and murdering helpless people in cold blood. The British were able to appreciate this, even if the Germans could not.

The French were not interested in the dialectics of atrocities. Logical as always they were simply in Operation *Musketeer* for what they could get out of it. Chief among their aims was the recovery of the Suez Canal. To this end collusion with Israel was a trivial, if important means.

Overhead at this moment was another logical Frenchman. Colonel de Fouquières was liaison officer to Admiral Barjot the French operational commander. He had instructions to find out at first-hand how the battle for the airfield was progressing and in particular whether the airfield was usable. From his circling Dakota he could see the main runway was clear. The Sappers of 9 Squadron had rolled away the oil drums blocking it soon after landing. The French Colonel ordered his pilot to land.

Regardless of the occasional mortar bombs still bursting on the airfield the Dakota swept down the runway, and taxied over to the control tower buildings. The pilot kept his engines running.

They would be flying straight back to Cyprus, and they had room for casualties on board. My French is pathetic, and against the spluttering harshness of the engines our conversation was brief.

'*Combien de bléssés pouvez-vous porter?*'

'*Huit.*' He held up eight fingers.

'*Et vous allez tout droit en Chypre?*'

'*Jusqu'a Akrotiri.*'

'*Alors. Dix minutes?*'

'*Bien Sur.*'

I went back to the garage to select the cases. It was invidious. They all ought to go. No one noticed as we walked the length of the building, picking a name here and there. Dick Stevens should go with his two wounds, the chest case which Norman and Malcolm had just completed, a mortar splinter in a knee joint, a shattered foot. This man had landed in a minefield on the shore.

The orderlies carried them carefully to the plane and fitted the stretchers on board.

One of the boys died just as the preparations were complete. His body was replaced with one in more urgent need of attention.

CHAPTER IX

FROM RUSSIA WITH LOVE

As we unstrapped the stretcher and carried it awkwardly out of the doorway, Tubby and the Brigade Major were standing by. The dead boy was our patient, but he was also their soldier, and their concern showed. It made our job a lot easier.

The Brigade Major looked dubiously at my eye and murmured something about 'getting another doctor.' He was nursing a mortar splinter in the tongue himself, but had not thought this worthy of mention.

It was Norman Kirby, the surgeon, who settled it. He made one of his periodic sorties from his operating theatre, to see how everything was going outside.

'Take this bottle' he said, pressing a pint of plasma into my hands 'and make sure that drip keeps running on the plane.' He turned as though to get on with the next case and added, seemingly as an afterthought:

'And I want someone to look at that eye.'

There was no point in arguing. The transfusion of the wounded man must be kept going at all costs and in my monocular state I was the most expendable member of the medical staff. I very much doubted whether there was much to be done for the eye. But it felt like desertion and I wandered round saying a few apologetic goodbyes.

'I wouldn't go walking around out there unless you have to,' said Malcolm Elliott, the anaesthetist, 'there's still an awful lot of muck flying about.'

Good old Malcolm, I thought, pessimistic to the last.

Which made his actions next day all the more remarkable.

156

I climbed onto the Dakota with the precious bottle of plasma and one or two items of personal kit which seemed worth salvaging from my ruined rucksack. Inside the aircraft there was a fine display of contrasts. The Frenchmen were immaculate in képis and perfectly pressed khaki drill uniform. Our wounded lay partly clad, many of them with shirts or trousers ruthlessly slashed so that dressings could be applied. The scarlet and yellow patches of their blood-soaked shell dressings glared against the olive green and khaki of their tattered clothes.

I looked out of the window as we taxied to the end of the runway. A drab afternoon had settled in. Part of the darkness was due to an overcast sky, to which the wreaths of black smoke winding up above Port Said made a sombre backcloth. But not all the gloom was outside. Looking around me in the aircraft I noted the similarity of size and structure between the Dakota and the Valetta in which I had flown a mere five hours ago. It seemed like five years. And my companions from the battalion, flying back to Cyprus, bore a sorry resemblance to that tense, poised stick of parachutists in the morning.

The pilot had no need to warm his engines. He revved them once at the west end of the runway and then we were away. Quickly the tail came off the ground as we gathered speed, and seconds later we were airborne past the control tower. To avoid A.A. fire over Port Said the pilot quickly wheeled northwards, and the sewage farm and cemetery slipped away beneath the starboard wing. We were ignorant of the drama being enacted below.

Helped by several very accurate air strikes, 'C' Company had fought on beyond the far end of the cemetery until they came under fire from a large block of flats. This was the western fringe of Port Said itself. The open ground in front of the flats contained three Russian S.U. 100 self-propelled guns, dug in so that they lay hull-down and well concealed. Thanks to the air strikes these had been abandoned by the Egyptians and were quickly overrun.

157

By now the score of captured enemy equipment was impressive. Besides the Russian self-propelled guns, which were tanks in all but fact, there were several mortars, two 3·7-inch A.A. guns, and a mass of machine guns and small arms of all sorts.

But one machine gun was still very much in enemy hands. From the bottom of the block of flats withering fire slashed over the sand towards the 'C' Company soldiers, who were forced to take cover.

What Mike Newall, our machine gun officer, was doing in the front line at this moment is obscure. He doubtless could have produced a convincing excuse—such as searching for a new position for his Vickers guns to enfilade the enemy position as 'C' Company went forward. Nevertheless it is unorthodox for medium machine-guns, or their commander, to lead an advance. But Mike, the whimsical, dreamy officer who had impersonated EOKA, would not have been considering details such as that. He could see that the advance was held up, and he could see the position of the enemy machine-gun in the flats. In no-man's-land he could also see an abandoned Bren-gun carrier among the litter of discarded Egyptian equipment. If it worked, the Bren-gun carrier was the answer to the problem.

He had a few quick words with the sergeant commanding the 'C' Company forward patrol. They dashed out through the enemy fire towards the Bren-gun carrier, and climbed in. For all his air of whimsy Mike could master mechanical problems easily. Later on, in a dull moment, he invented a simple means of zeroing the '106' anti-tank gun which saved the War Office countless precious rounds of ammunition.

The carrier started at the first attempt. Mike and the sergeant drove it straight at the enemy position, which was routed. Then they returned in triumph down the road, back towards the airfield and our own lines.

It was not quite clear where our own lines were at the time. After the cemetery had been cleared by 'C' Company considerable opposition was still directed at them from houses and ditches along the road to their left. Mike Walsh and Dennis Beckett the second-in-command of the battalion had come forward during the afternoon to confer with the Colonel among the tombstones. As they left the cemetery gate they were pinned down by a sniper a hundred yards up the road towards Port Said. Mike Walsh fired a few rounds with his Sten gun, which then jammed. But Dennis had got back to cover before it did so. Mike Walsh felt very vulnerable as he ran back to rejoin him, without getting hit.

Therefore, as Mike Newall and the sergeant drove their captured Bren-gun carrier back along the road, everyone was alert. The movement of an enemy armoured vehicle was reported by wireless to the 'cab-rank' of Venoms circling overhead. But the pilot of the leading aircraft radioed back that he couldn't see any armour moving on the ground. It may be that by this time the Bren-gun carrier had reached a patch of bushes near the cemetery wall.

The anti-tank detachment with 'B' Company had been brought forward by Bill Hill to cover the cemetery battle. Suddenly the Number One gunner spotted the Bren-gun carrier moving jerkily through the bushes, about a hundred yards away. It could only be an enemy vehicle. Two spotting rounds were fired quickly to get the range.

The second one hit the carrier square in the middle. They were certain to score a hit with the main armament.

'Don't shoot! That's Mr. Newall!' came the distraught voice of Sergeant Howse of the machine-gun platoon. He had seen it all coming and had run up and shouted his warning with half a second to spare.

Mike, who had been grinning like a fiend when he passed the 'C' Company headquarters along the road was ignorant of his escape. He and Bill Hill had a somewhat sheepish encounter when they met later.

And the Bren-gun carrier joined the increasing quantity of 'liberated' Egyptian transport back at the airfield.

As the Dakota climbed away northwards, back towards

Cyprus, the passengers were mostly beyond caring about the problems left behind on the ground. They had their troubles with them.

A pool of blood had accumulated on the floor. I looked for its source. This turned out to be the shattered foot of the boy who had landed on a mine. I tightened another field dressing on top of the three already there. Further up the aircraft was Dick Stevens, still having a lot of pain from his leg. He asked for a cigarette.

'I'll never say a word against the Colonel again,' he said, as I held the flickering lighter. 'Always thought he was only a Staff Officer. But today he was first class. Left us to run our own show and always there to help.' His drawn face sagged into repose, and for a while he dozed.

The Frenchmen were splendid, and generous with good wishes and help. Considering they were not a medical outfit, but an offshoot of the General Staff we were indeed fortunate.

Some of the boys wanted a drink. I approached Colonel de Fouquières.

'*Est ce qu'il y a de l'eau?*'

'*Mais oui.*'

And he sent one of his aides back with me to the lavatory in the tail of the aircraft. There was enough to give everyone who wanted it a sip or two. The transfusion kept running precariously. And the grey sea slid past in slow motion far beneath us.

Somewhere below was the invasion fleet, gathering for the sea assault on Port Said next morning. The hammer was about to fall, but 3 PARA and the Frenchmen had cracked the nut first.

And somewhere in the sky to the west of us the second 3 PARA lift flew towards El Gamil airfield, as the second lift of Frenchmen flew in to Port Fuad on the east side of the Suez Canal. Both the French and British troops on the ground welcomed the sight of reinforcements and more supplies being dropped to them.

The two R.A.F. men who had jumped with 3 PARA arranged the Dropping Zone markings for the second lift. Flight Lieutenant Roe was the officer in charge. Stan Roe was the inconspicuous type of R.A.F. officer, quiet, modest and with an all-prevailing sense of fun. A few days ago we had sat together painting our names on our cases and boxes before they were handed in to Bob Grainger's store in camp. Stan had taken his coming job philosophically. Not every R.A.F. officer would relish being dumped in the middle of a battle on the ground with a parachute battalion, but to Stan it had apparently been routine, like laying out flares for a drop on Frensham Common. During the battle for El Gamil airfield Stan was said to have been found sitting on a container working out the correct pay and allowances for one day as Air Officer Commanding Egypt. Being the only R.A.F. officer aground in Port Said at the time he might well have got away with them as his just entitlement. This rumour was unfortunately never substantiated. Stan's sense of humour never affected his thoroughness. Parachuting to him, as to all R.A.F. instructors was not, in the end, a subject of fun. They did too much of it to take it lightly, and their very livelihood and promotion depended on doing it well.

He and the Sergeant Parachute Jumping Instructor with him had been thorough with their Dropping Zone markings. The sodium flares were ignited in plenty of time for the pilots to run in on them to drop their sticks. With one single exception it all went perfectly.

The exception was Corporal Brackpool of the Pay Staff. He was standing in the door of a Valetta as the aircraft crossed the coast. Suddenly a mile west of the dropping point the aircraft banked steeply. With his heavy weapon container he was caught off guard and fell out. As the lone parachute was spotted in the distance a great cheer went up from the troops on the airfield.

But it was not as funny as all that. Brackpool landed in the sea, the far side of the broken El Gamil bridge. He had to abandon most of his clothes and equipment to cross from the sandbank on the west side of the channel. He had waded ashore on this sandspit after landing, alone and unarmed. A party of Egyptians appeared from nowhere among the sand dunes, determined to finish him off.

The Officers' Mess Sergeant was despatched with a patrol from battalion headquarters to retrieve him. Sergeant Vokes had made a most efficient barman in Tunisia Camp and could produce a brandy sour or John Collins unobtrusively, as though he had it up his sleeve all the time, and the infuriating complexities of Mess bills were simple to him. He now made an equally competent patrol commander. On their way over the sand dunes his patrol came under fire from a pillbox which had somehow escaped attention earlier on. They attacked and destroyed this strongpoint, killing two of its defenders and taking several prisoners. With great relief all round they finally joined up with Brackpool coming to meet them in his underwear. He was able to make good his shortage of clothes and weapons with captured Egyptian equipment when he arrived at the control tower.

The Dakota crossed the coast of Cyprus near Akrotiri and we began to lose height on the let-down to Nicosia. Soon, in the gathering dusk, the airfield appeared below and we banked for the approach. As the wheels thumped and screeched on the runway I remembered, disbelievingly, that I had left it only twelve hours ago.

The fullest twelve hours of my life.

We taxied over to the concrete apron on the perimeter track near the north edge of the camp. Tunisia Camp was only a few hundred yards away, but now it seemed like a different, forgotten world.

On the concrete stood several ambulances and quite a reception party. There were numerous medical orderlies and an R.A.M.C. Colonel in charge. I climbed down the ladder and explained roughly what the casualties on board were. Meanwhile kind ladies of Nicosia milled around us dispensing tea and sympathy. Most of us could do with quantities of both. But I had to dissuade them from filling up with fluid some of the boys who were obviously due to be given a general anaesthetic shortly.

The Colonel came back with me and his experienced eye glowered round.

'Get a helicopter,' he rapped out to an orderly in the background.

Next moment, with the familiar searing of rotors overhead, a helicopter landed alongside. The patient with the chest wound was transferred gently to it and the transfusion bottle handed in after him. In a blast of dust and noise they were off, riding smoothly above the bumpy roads, straight to the Military Hospital.

Where he survived just another thirty-six hours.

The remaining wounded were transferred to ambulances. I said a grateful goodbye to Colonel de Fouquières and the Dakota took off back to Akrotiri.

'You come with me,' said the R.A.M.C. Colonel, and we drove in silence to the hospital, round the old city of Nicosia, past the familiar houses and streets of the suburbs. Now that it was all over there was somehow not much to be said.

In the suburbs of Port Said it was far from over. As darkness descended, the Colonel conferred with Tubby Butler at the edge of the cemetery. The battalion had done its job well, perhaps too well. For they could not be certain that the ground on which they stood was not among the targets for the Naval bombardment next morning. And so for the night 'C' Company withdrew back from the cemetery to the eastern edge of the airfield, leaving 'B' Company to hold the front in their positions at the forward end of the sewage farm.

At the same time news came by wireless from the Frenchmen near the Ferdan Bridge. Colonel Conan, their commander, had been in touch by telephone with the Egyptian Commandant of Port Said. He hoped that a Cease Fire might be arranged, and had ordered all strafing by fighter aircraft to end at 1700 hours. Tubby and the Brigade Major flew over by helicopter to join the French at the southern edge of the town. Surrender terms would have to be decided by the High Command.

And now, when rapid communication and decision might have saved the day, enabling a Cease Fire to be negotiated quickly, the communications failed. It was just over sixteen years since the wireless failure at Arnhem had contributed to the costly disaster there. Now, when the fate of the Suez Canal, and it could be, indirectly, the fate of the Western World also, were in the balance the wirelesses again failed to make contact. The years between had seen prodigious expenditure on weapons of all sorts. Nuclear bombs, supersonic aircraft and guided missiles existed in profusion.

There was delay while the report was relayed to General Stockwell offshore, and further delay while he in turn made contact with General Keightley, the Operational Commander. Inevitably there was delay while surrender terms were drawn up. The Egyptian Commander was anxious to surrender but could not do so without authority from Cairo. He was given time to get this but unfortunately the Russian Consul, by talk of Russian help and rocket attacks on London and Paris, persuaded him to fight on. Cairo confirmed this decision.

In their positions around the airfield 3 PARA were ignorant of all this. They only knew that from 1800 hours to 2030 hours an uneasy cease fire held sway.

Karl Beale commanding 'B' Company was sharing a slit trench with his sergeant-major. All the slit trenches in that low-lying sandy ground had become waterlogged, so that they sat outside chatting. The sergeant-major was a veteran and had been through all this sort of thing long ago. Karl, despite the Military Cross he had won in Malaya, had not been soldiering for very long. This was his first operational jump and his thirteenth in all, and he said as much.

'That's odd, sir,' said the sergeant-major, 'my first op. jump

164

was my thirteenth too. That was the Rhine Crossing. Now that *was* a party.'

To which Karl could find no reply.

During the Cease Fire two mortar bombardments came over from the Egyptian lines. The first landed in the sea on the left of 'B' Company, and the second in the lake on their right. The company made no answer.

The mosquitoes infesting the sewage farm knew no cease fire rules at all. Chris Hogg and his platoon could not get their own appalling stench out of their nostrils, and the vicious mosquito bites added to their misery. A fortnight later, when they had returned to Cyprus, many of them still bore the marks of that wretched night.

On the seaward edge of the short front line was Pompey Norman's platoon. Hearing a noise to their front in the middle of the night they all stood-to. It sounded like an enemy patrol approaching. When the noise seemed to be about twenty-five yards away Pompey ordered his Bren-gunner to fire. He let off a long burst, after which there was silence and the rest of the night passed peacefully. In the light of dawn the 'patrol' turned out to have been a horse which now lay, quite still, with its legs sticking up in the air.

During the long night Jim Burke the Intelligence Officer was sent down from Battalion Headquarters with a message for 'B' Company. In the thick darkness he walked straight through the front line without noticing it. Eventually he realised his mistake and returned from no man's land. He was lucky not to meet the same fate as the horse.

It was not quiet in Port Said itself. The distant crackle of small-arms fire disturbed the night air. This was all the work of one man.

Anatoli Tchikov, the Russian Consul in Port Said had been slow on the draw. Among other things, he was responsible for disposing of the enormous quantities of arms and ammunition shipped to Port Said in the last few months from countries behind the Iron Curtain. The correct disposal and use of this equipment must in fact have been his chief task, for he had no Russian citizens to deal with in Port Said, only one Russian Canal pilot, known as 'The Admiral'.

He had failed to distribute his arms during the bombing phase preceding the landings. And even the considerate action of the Anglo-French forces in broadcasting their warning to civilians in Port Said had not aroused him. Surely this direct hint over Cyprus Radio the previous evening might have been taken? Tchikov must have thought his prospects of winning the Russian equivalent of the O.B.E. were poor that morning of 5th November as he saw the French and British parachutists pouring out onto their Dropping Zones.

But over the next few days he excelled himself. He perceived, with the same clarity as Grivas had done in Cyprus, that the children were his best allies. The senior students and even young schoolchildren were wildly, fanatically pro-Nasser. He could see that the Egyptian Army was a poorly-officered rabble, incapable of co-ordinated action. Perhaps memories of what he had seen or heard of the Battle of Stalingrad during the war inspired him. There a whole German army had floundered to a halt in merciless street fighting in which guerrillas had played an important part.

With enough guerrillas shooting on his side he just might achieve the same sort of success here.

A rallying cry was needed, so he mobilised loud-speaker vans which toured the streets.

'Fight on people of Port Said! Russian help is coming! Tonight London and Paris will be destroyed with atomic rockets!'

It may have seemed improbable, but it was enough to confirm the waverers. The vast supplies of machine guns, carbines and ammunition were issued to all who would take them. There was no time for weapon training, but to Tchikov that did not matter. The lives of the sundry civilians, and teenagers who composed his forces were expendable.

And tonight, in the distant streets of Port Said many were

being expended. Far from any real enemies the Egyptian boys fondled their new playthings. Accidents were frequent and they mistook bursts of fire among themselves for parties of parachutists. The children's War developed into a campaign all of its own.

Norman Kirby operated on many Egyptians and removed a large number of bullets from soldiers and civilians of all ages during the next few days. None of the bullets was British.

In the British Military Hospital in Nicosia the staff set about the task of repairing the damage to our own wounded. As the R.A.M.C. Colonel and I drove through the guarded outer gateway I had to tell myself forcibly that I had been in here less than twenty-four hours ago, looking for the injured Sapper. All that fuss about Security now seemed a little overdone. I lost touch of the other soldiers from the battalion and was transferred to the care of the ophthalmologist. He gave my eye a most comprehensive overhaul, picked a fragment of metal off the cornea and pronounced the internal damage to be comparatively trivial. With rest it should all settle down. I felt more of a fraud than ever as I climbed in between clean sheets in the officers' ward. I bundled all my personal belongings into the bedside locker.

Next morning I pulled them out and there was my wretched automatic pistol, cocked and loaded, with a round ready to fire in the chamber. It was a miracle I hadn't shot someone by accident since that futile volley I had fired on El Gamil airfield.

But on the airfield itself there was more drama than this, as dawn broke on 6th November. The battalion was observing the traditional dawn 'stand-to'. Offshore, the sea armada approached the shore and the landing craft began their run-in to the beaches. Overhead, waves of Fleet Air Arm Venoms and Sea Hawks dived again and again in support of the beach landings.

Geoff Norton stood with his sergeant-major near the west end of the runway watching it all. Suddenly he noticed a plane weaving in beneath the rest, in the opposite direction. It was coming straight at them from the direction of Port Said.

'Look at that idiot, he'll get hit by the others if he doesn't watch it,' said Geoff.

As he spoke, lines of green and white tracer came bouncing down the runway towards them. Geoff felt mesmerised by the pretty, unusual colours of the bullets. But instinct won, and his next memory was of having the wind knocked out of him as the sergeant-major landed on top of him in a nearby slit trench.

The Mig fighter, with Egyptian markihgs on its wings, roared low overhead and disappeared to the west. This solitary appearance by the Egyptian Air Force was denied by our own Intelligence service. But to prove the point the Mig reappeared later in the morning and strafed the airfield again, causing one casualty.

As this occurred 'C' Company were under orders to reoccupy the cemetery. The platoon commanders were annoyed more by having to abandon their breakfast, uneaten, on the command 'prepare to move' than by the strafing, which was over and gone before they realised what was happening.

Noel Hodgson was angry, too, but for a different reason. His company headquarters was near the wall at the west end of the airfield and it was surrounded by various stores. 'D' Company was responsible for collecting and distributing the quantities of ammunition and supplies which had been dropped with the two air lifts yesterday. Everything of value on the airfield had been collected into this area.

Shrouded in blankets, among the valuable equipment, lay the bodies of two 3 PARA soldiers awaiting burial.

The wireless network was quiet for a moment and Noel's signaller had played with the frequency, so that the wireless set was receiving a news bulletin direct from the B.B.C. in London. The '52' set was capable of great feats of reception when it didn't matter. On one occasion later, in Jordan, we could hear Beethoven's Violin Concerto from the Albert Hall with perfect clarity, when the company twenty miles down the road was out of contact.

Through the earphones, audible to the staff of the 'D' Company headquarters grouped around, the news came crackling over. There was an opening report about the 'heavy fighting' in which the battalion had been embroiled on Port Said airfield. Then the distant voice went on to describe the uproar in Parliament, the frenzied, undignified scenes as the politicians argued, much too late, about the rights and wrongs of the action.

For Noel it was too much. All this indecision and discussion being reported smugly, remotely. Behind him, the two boys' bodies lay as mute reminders of the cost to the battalion, while democracy slowly made up its mind.

One of his soldiers evidently felt the same.

'What a shower of bastards what's for breakfast?' he said in one flat, heartfelt sentence, and firmly turned the wireless set back onto the correct frequency.

There was more fighting to be done.

As the landing craft ran in to land, the 3 PARA medium machine-guns gave covering fire along the beaches. The Commandos touched down on the sandy shore where opposition was slight. But as they moved into the town unpleasant street fighting developed. One Commando was landed by helicopter further inland, and the break-out southwards from Port Said seemed to be assured.

'C' Company pressed forward again, through the cemetery. From the blocks of flats and the Coastguard barracks on the outskirts of the town there was a lot of sniping. These buildings must be cleared before the company could join forces with the Commandos in the town beyond.

Ron Norman laid on a careful attack by two platoons which captured the buildings without suffering loss themselves. And by 0800 hours the Colonel was able to report his immediate mission completed.

'What next?' he enquired by wireless.

'A' Company lay back in reserve, ready to advance south-wards down the Canal if the need arose. But throughout the morning it appeared that the Marine Commandos were encountering considerable opposition in the town. Between 'C' Company and the Marines lay a hospital, a large expanse of shanty town and a police barracks. An advance through this area was ordered.

The main road forked at the outskirts of Port Said and the hospital lay in the arms of the fork. To the left lay a few buildings alongside the open beaches, and to the right was shanty town with the police barracks away to the south, across a hundred yards of open ground.

It fell to Jack Richardson to lead a fighting patrol forward, in an attempt to link up with the Commandos. Jack was not one to give up lightly. He would rub his nose against a problem before considering it seriously, and the nose sometimes got bloody in the process.

Most of the opposition was centred in shanty town and the police barracks, but a machine-gun had been sited in the far end of the hospital buildings. The patrol moved by bounds along the few buildings to the left of the road. At the last building the desultory fire directed at them became intense.

Jack Richardson looked over a low wall and ducked as a bullet smacked close by. He looked at his beret. A great score was gouged out of the crown near the badge.

'A bloody sight too close for comfort,' he said to Private Penning who was with him. Penning agreed.

They worked along the wall towards the lee of the hospital buildings and dashed across the road. A jump and a snatch took them over the high wall surrounding the hospital grounds.

In the buildings themselves was a scene of pathetic chaos. On the second floor all the seriously ill patients were still in, or under, their beds, obviously terrified. The staff had left them to their fate. As British parachutists swarmed into the wards they must have felt the worst was at hand.

It was, but from their compatriots across the road to the south. From the police barracks and shanty town the Egyptians poured all the fire they could muster through the windows and doorways. Penning was hit in the hand by two machine-gun bullets. His friends bound up the wounds and dropped him over the wall at the back, into the road again, where for the moment he was out of trouble.

Port Said is first and foremost a place of trade. Even during the battle the tradition died hard. As 'C' Company were fighting desperately into the outskirts of the town, Geoff Norton commanding Support Company stood in the cemetery behind them. From among the shattered tombstones an Egyptian civilian approached him, heedless of the stray bullets cracking around. He produced a crumpled collection of papers from his pocket. These were references from a number of British regiments to whom he had served as contractor in the old days in the Canal Zone. He asked if, as he was the first, he might secure the privilege of acting as contractor to 3 PARA? To seal the bargain did Geoff fancy a nice little bint as well? The references were all endorsed in similar vein, testifying that he was the biggest rogue this side of the Sweetwater canal and should, if possible, be shot on sight or words to that effect.

At this moment Jack Richardson and the men with him were trying to avoid being shot on sight. But unsuccessfully.

They had crossed over into the nearest houses on the shanty town side of the road. With Jack was Sergeant Read, a tall, fair-haired young man with a vivid personality and boundless drive. Although he was only on a short service engagement he had quickly risen from private soldier to sergeant and was one of the most popular N.C.O.'s in the company. Every man felt that 'Lofty' Read, who had so recently been a private himself, understood the Toms' point of view, and his example was one they could all emulate. Corporal Stead was the third man. Reliable, calm and unemotional, he had naturally teamed up with the other two as they pushed forward.

171

Jack rounded the corner of the house and saw a blur hurtling straight at him. He twisted sideways. The rocket-launcher bomb hit his rifle and knocked it flying, together with the tips of three of his fingers. He looked at the bloody pulp which remained and was surprised at the lack of pain. In a detached way he wondered why the bomb had failed to explode.

At the same instant Corporal Stead's left arm was shattered by a bullet which hit him just above the elbow.

They fell back into the shelter of the house. It did not seem that any of them were going to get out of here alive.

Ron Norman was following this attack up with his company headquarters. They moved forward carefully and had to take cover repeatedly in ditches by the roadside as snipers opened up on them from cover at either side. Even so he was found at one moment by Jim Burke, standing quite still in the middle of the road in full view of the enemy, calmly surveying the scene with his binoculars.

Through them he could get a good idea of the desperate plight of the patrol ahead. He was beginning to work out a scheme for extricating them when, to his amazement, up drove the doctor in his jeep.

This was Malcolm Elliott.

CHAPTER X

MESS AND BOTCH

A KEEN Naval anaesthetist had come ashore by helicopter to lend a hand. He was immediately enrolled to give an anaesthetic for Norman Kirby's next case, while Malcolm attended to the problems of resuscitation and equipment. Supplies of all sorts were running low, and it was essential to get hold of more anaesthetics and more dressings.

Malcolm walked over to the Battalion Headquarters wireless set to find out what was going on. Gerald Mullins was receiving messages from Ron Norman's Company H.Q. along the road. Malcolm heard the welcome news that the forward troops were in a hospital whose staff had vanished. The very place for an anaesthetic machine! He explained what he wanted to do to Gerald, and borrowed his jeep and driver.

They drove merrily down the road towards Port Said and presently met the Colonel. Malcolm stopped and explained his purpose and then drove on. He passed the 'C' Company headquarters and noted with pleasure the friendly waving of the soldiers as he drove by. Further along was the hospital, in the fork of the road.

Under the wall surrounding the hospital buildings were a few more of 'C' Company. These were men of Jack Richardson's platoon who were tending the wounds of Private Penning. They waved vigorously at the M.O. driving past them, attempting to stop him before he headed straight into the Egyptian positions a short distance down the road.

Malcolm and his driver went straight on.

The machine-gun in the far end of the hospital itself finally checked them. It opened fire at about fifty yards range, and bullets smacked all around. Malcolm thought that this was much closer to the sharp end of the battle than he had ever intended. He felt furious at being fired at from the hospital precincts as the jeep turned and drove at top speed back towards the shelter of the wall.

It may have been un-sporting of the Egyptian machine gunner to set up his weapon in the hospital itself. But in that close, confused fighting the elastic rules of war were stretched to their limit.

What upset our soldiers more than this was the manner in which certain Labour members of Parliament later stretched the rules of Parliamentary privilege. It was insinuated that the heavy Egyptian casualties in Port Said were due to flagrant and callous violation of the Geneva Convention by our own forces. To troops who had been denied the usual preliminary bombardment of their objective, and whose enemies had expressly been warned to expect their attack both in time and place, these arguments rang somewhat hollow. It was not their fault that the assault on Port Said was pressed forward against the majority of world opinion and against considerable opposition at home. To mollify those who opposed the action much had been done to save Egyptian lives and sacrifice their own. To receive, as a final pat on the back, the accusation of wanton killing and destruction seemed ludicrous.

When Malcolm returned to the 'C' Company soldiers under the high wall things seemed pretty bad there also.

'You've just been through the front line,' he was told. By this time he had guessed as much himself. The soldiers told him that Jack Richardson and the others had crossed the road towards shanty town and become trapped by cross-fire, some of it from the hospital itself. Communication with them was almost impossible and at this time their true plight was not known.

Malcolm was the only officer present and, although he was a non-combatant, the soldiers naturally looked to him for advice. This seemed to be a military rather than a medical problem, so he drove back in the jeep to report to Ron Norman at the Company Headquarters two hundred yards to the rear. While Ron laid plans to relieve Jack's platoon, Malcolm returned to the hospital, driving himself this time, intending to pass on the news.

When he arrived he was told that several of the party across the road had been wounded. That was different. They were his responsibility now.

He drove across the road to where they were pinned down. The appalling clatter of small-arms fire and rocket-launcher bombs which were directed at him did not seem to deter him for a moment. Alongside a wall on the other side of the road he was once more under cover and he parked the jeep. In the house was Corporal Stead, severely wounded, and Jack Richardson with his shattered finger tips. Malcolm bound up their wounds and helped Corporal Stead into the jeep. He would have to drive back through that murderous fire again, and by now the enemy would be expecting him.

And now he discovered that he did not know where the reverse gear on a jeep was situated. Every gear he tried only made the vehicle take a short bound forward towards the Egyptian positions. In a yard or two more he would be out of the cover of the wall.

He talked to Sergeant Read, who was the only member of the patrol not wounded. There was nothing else for it. He would make a U-turn while the sergeant gave covering fire with his Bren gun.

The sergeant came out of the house and fired a long burst from the hip. Malcolm revved the engine and tore the jeep round as tightly as he could, back down the road. He left the wounded corporal at the 'C' Company headquarters. No one who watched him go in the hail of well-directed fire thought he had a hope of getting through.

He discussed it with Ron. Most of the fire appeared to have been coming from the police barracks away to the south of the road. An air-strike seemed to be the best solution. But by now it was late on November 6th and the political overtones of the

175

operation were becoming louder. Ron's wireless message was answered with the report that henceforth air-strikes had been called off 'to avoid further damage to civilian property'.

The only supporting weapon which could replace an air-strike was the '106'. The anti-tank detachment with 'C' Company had not yet fired their weapon in anger. They had been interested, if a little disappointed, to find that the Russian S.U.100 self-propelled guns did not need their attention. For by this time the guns had been abandoned by their crews for twenty-four hours. The anti-tank detachment moved forward to give what help they could to the beleaguered platoon in the region of the hospital.

Malcolm had developed quite a feeling for the military life by now and had returned in his jeep to the hospital. He intended to tell those who remained there that covering fire would soon be laid on. But the news which greeted him put the thought temporarily out of mind. Sergeant Read had been killed, just after firing that burst from the hip which enabled Malcolm and Corporal Stead to get away. Malcolm questioned the sergeant's companions carefully. There was no doubt about it. He had been hit by a bullet in the groin and bled profusely. In a matter of seconds he had collapsed and died in the arms of one of the boys with him. His pulse had gone.

It did not seem worth risking the cross-fire to fetch his body back from the other side of the road.

In the friendly closeness of the platoon and company, scattered as they were, this bad news spread swiftly as smoke. Gloom struck all who heard it. Private Penning, on his way back past the Company Headquarters, found an Irish corporal weeping unashamedly. His friend Lofty was dead.

But tears were not going to save those who were left behind at the hospital. The '106' anti-tank gun crew brought their weapon forward and quickly spotted the enemy positions in shanty town and the police barracks.

They fired just five rounds.

It was more effective than they had dared to hope. The

police barracks was shattered and wreathed in great spongy
billows of smoke. The shacks of shantytown blew apart into so
much tinder, as the powerful explosions burst among them.
And like tinder they went up in flames. The enemy cross-fire
withered away to nothing. Shantytown was ablaze.

But the sergeant had not died. As he lay unconscious from
that catastrophic loss of blood, his pulse, impalpable to his
friends, was still beating. Lying down helps. It lessens bleeding from leg wounds, and raises the blood pressure slightly in
the brain, enough to produce consciousness. And so it was
with him. The confusing, wet, painful mist cleared. Rat-tat-
tat! Machine-gun fire, and close too. Funny smell. Rat-tat-
tat!

Fire! The machine gun was the crackling flames in the
room where he lay. He could not walk. He must crawl or be
burnt alive.

He crawled. One leg was useless, so he dragged it behind
him. Out of the doorway and left-handed, back along the road.
A few slow yards and the mist overwhelmed him again. He
blacked out. When it cleared once more some Egyptian
civilians were bending over, spitting on him. But they did not
kill him. He crawled on, for his will to live was very strong,
and his instinct of self preservation stronger still. Then he
blacked out for a second time. When he came to an Egyptian
soldier appeared pointing a carbine.

So this was the end. Humane killing. A shot in the head at
point-blank range. But his mind although it was barely
conscious worked quicker than the Egyptian's. A grenade! He
hadn't any but he went through the motions of throwing one.
The Egyptian fled.

This was not the last danger. Crawling back from the enemy
lines, in the dusk, he was certain to get finished off by a burst of
fire from his own friends in 'C' Company. For unobtrusively,
unnoticed by them all, the night had almost fallen. He brought
out his handkerchief and waved it intermittently as he
crawled on.

Ron Norman was standing at his company headquarters with Malcolm Elliott and Horace McClelland. Morale was low. The platoon had been severely mauled in the hospital, and one of the best 'C' Company sergeants was lost.

Then somebody called out that he had seen a white flag waving along the road. Several years later Ron, describing that moment, could hardly restrain his relief.

'About eight of us dashed forward,' he said, 'and by God it was him!'

From ground level the sergeant did not know who was rushing at him out of the gathering darkness. He did not even know whether they were friends or foes till he saw one was carrying a blackthorn stick.

'Thank God for that,' he thought, 'it can only be the padre.'

And they carried him in.

Malcolm was at a loss for words, as they tended to his wounds.

'I'm terribly sorry, sergeant,' he said, 'we thought you were dead.' Meaning that he would have gone back for him again, had there been a hope of his being alive.

The sergeant was too weak and shocked to be impressed by this, or any other, argument.

'After all,' said Malcolm later, 'what *do* you say to someone whom you believe to be dead when he crawls out of a building to which *you've* set fire?'

To which few of us will ever need to find an answer.

However disparagingly Malcolm might view his own efforts, the powers-that-be thought otherwise. His gallantry in rescuing Corporal Stead, and helping to extricate the other 'C' Company soldiers was recognised by the award of the Military Cross. Sergeant Read was awarded the Military Medal for his part in the action. His crawl from beyond the grave, from cremation itself, inspired them all that night. The low spirits of 'C' Company soared once more.

Night was falling. An end had come to the second day of fighting in Port Said. The battalion had been in action for forty-eight hours since taking off from Nicosia, and the prospect of rest was welcome.

The drama of Operation *Musketeer* was not confined to Port Said. Its repercussions had shaken Cairo, Tel Aviv, Paris and London. Now, as darkness fell over the Middle East the Great Powers took a hand. In Washington the pound sterling was subjected to financial pressure which threatened to ruin the British economy. And from Moscow came a different, more sinister threat. Tass published Bulganin's letter addressed to the French and British heads of Government. This requested the immediate cessation of hostilities, and alluded to Russian atomic missiles which could reach London and Paris.

It was a clever move, cleverly timed. The semi-official publication of these veiled threats via a news agency was sure to have an enormous international impact. The official documents delivered later bore no direct threats at all. But the rumour was enough to give a veneer of truth to Tchikov's cynical proclamations as his loudspeakers toured the streets of Port Said. Enough to make the soldiers pause before they turned a blind eye to their orders.

For orders had come through for a Cease Fire to become effective at 23.59 hours on November 6th. Regardless of what the soldiers felt, the politicians had had enough.

The soldiers' feelings were mixed. They would not be sorry to stop this rotten business, but they could see, more clearly than anyone else, how little they had yet achieved. It was tantalising. To the south of Port Said the way lay open to Ismailia and Suez.

Despite Tubby's protestations 2 PARA, who were to lead the advance southwards, were not allowed to disembark until dark. They were originally due to land in the morning. Now, with a squadron of tanks they fought their way through Port Said.

Tubby Butler had joined the leading tanks as they advanced along the Canal Road. Characteristically he had attached himself to the spearhead of the attack. By midnight they had reached El Cap nineteen miles down the Canal. The majority of the waterway remained in Egyptian hands.

This was an opportunity the Egyptians did not overlook. Aided and abetted by the Admiral, the Russian Canal pilot, they scuttled blockships at either end of the Canal and sank some forty ships in it. The destruction was complete and thorough.

In 3 PARA's end of Port Said there was an impressive amount of destruction also. The night sky was aglow with the flames of shanty town as the battalion settled down for their second night ashore in Egypt. 'C' Company had the awkward job of maintaining the front line in the region of the hospital. 'B' Company moved up into the blocks of flats behind them.

Battalion Headquarters spent the night in a building which, in retrospect, turned out to have been a brothel. All its human inmates had fled, but behind them they had left legions of the most vicious fleas. Everyone who slept there itched for days afterwards.

The battalion's transport force had been greatly enlarged. Vehicles of all sorts had swelled the ranks, and during the fighting one of the Russian *S.U.*100's had joined them. This was thanks to the efforts of the Turk. Sergeant Turkiewicz had spent some time in tanks during the war, and after tinkering with the self-propelled gun for a short time he drove it proudly out of the pit where it had been abandoned. It gave useful service during the subsequent occupation of Port Said by 3 PARA and the Colonel was able to tour his sector of the town riding on the turret.

But in the darkness the Colonel was unable to travel round his battalion area. In the front line, despite the Cease Fire, sporadic bursts of fire still came from the Egyptian positions. And stray snipers were active in the area round the blocks of flats. Thanks to the veiled threats from Moscow the Colonel had no doubt where his responsibilities lay. It was not for 3 PARA to continue fighting against these pinprick enemies if thereby they might precipitate a major nuclear war.

The news bulletins also reached us in the officer's ward in British Military Hospital Nicosia. News, in one form or another, had occupied much of the patients' day there. Early in the morning a liaison officer had come in.

'I've a couple of Press Correspondents outside,' he said, 'would you mind if they came in and had a word with you?'

Dick Stevens, lying up the other end of the ward was clearly in no state to be bothered with this sort of thing.

'All right,' I said.

And in walked a whole platoon of correspondents. Men, women, photographers, they crowded round the bed. A black patch covered my right eye and the scene must have looked like an exhausted pirate king briefing his rascals.

The questions pelted in from all sides and I answered them as best I could. What subsequently appeared in the papers bore no relation to what had happened on El Gamil airfield.

'I was so sorry to read all that humiliating tripe,' an uncle wrote to my father afterwards. 'If a chap can't get hit without becoming a public show, it's a poor look-out.'

Uncle Tom had fought through two world wars, and in consequence held fairly definite views on how casualties should be treated. It was thanks to the efforts of his generation that our casualties at Port Said were comparatively light. For commanders today value the lives of their men more than ever before. This is due in large measure to the carnage of the Somme, Ypres and those four hopeless years whose youth was harvested in the First War. Every General since those days has been haunted by the memory, and has vowed subconsciously that it shall not happen again.

Yet, paradoxically, if a generation had not vanished as a dream in 1914–18 we might not have attacked Port Said at all. The Prime Minister, Eden, was a survivor of the lost generation himself. He had lived to see his children's generation withered in the Second World War and he did not want to see their successors blighted in the Third. To him Nasser was as likely to cause the Third World War as Hitler had been the instigator of the Second.

He was wrong. Arabs, luckily for us, are not Germans. But it was an honest and brave mistake.

It was also tragic. As the battalion in Port Said faced the dawn of their third day there, they could get some idea of the vastness of the tragedy.

On the airfield regrets were domestic, personal. Horace McClelland was conducting a burial service for the three soldiers of the battalion who had been killed there. As he was concluding the prayers a Tom arrived from 'B' Company. He stood beside the third grave, his beret in his hand.

There was a pause.

'He was my mate,' he said. And with a terrible, bursting sob, went off, back to his company.

Comedy reared its head from time to time. At dawn a lonely Valetta had circled the airfield for fifteen minutes, requesting permission to land. Its fighter escort had to return to Cyprus meanwhile to refuel. Stan Roe, the Air Officer Commanding Egypt, who was acting Station Commander, was having a well-earned rest. He was rudely awakened with a message that the Air Officer Commanding Levant was overhead. Would he please give permission for the Valetta to touch down?

A tousled figure, battle dress hastily pulled on over pyjamas, was said to have been seen running to the Control Tower. The green Verey light was fired in the nick of time.

The battalion rapidly became infiltrated by a lot of Top Brass. The soldiers were struck by the contrast between the arrival of the senior officers and their own descent on the airfield two days ago. Seeing a neat, well-dressed figure climbing down from the Valetta, they wondered, irreverently, whether he was going to shout 'Taxi' or 'Porter'.

But, however incongruous their arrival might seem to their men, the Commanders had pressing problems on hand. Generals Keightley and Stockwell conferred at the control tower and looked round the airfield and the overthrown

Egyptian defences. Later in the morning they toured the town.

There was much to be done.

3 PARA had endured sporadic Egyptian fire since daybreak. Much of this was from civilians, or soldiers who had deemed it prudent to don civilian clothes. Pacifying this end of Port Said was to present a continual problem to Allied forces during the occupation. It was in this area that the unfortunate Lieutenant Moorhouse later met his end. In the early morning the battalion linked up, first of all with a patrol from I PARA which had come along the beach, and later with Marine Commandos who were to occupy the next section eastwards.

The battalion was given the task of maintaining law and order in their sector, which included the ground between the airfield and the hospital. They were also to help the 9 Squadron Sappers to rebuild the broken El Gamil bridge, and collect what arms they could find.

So they had to make good the damage which they and their supporting arms had caused only forty-eight hours earlier. Which set them thinking. One of the subalterns later described it all as the most fantastically sickening and disillusioning experience of his life. Many of his soldiers would have agreed with him. For however much damage the 'children's war' and the callous, cynical, distribution of Russian arms had caused, there was no doubt that much of what had occurred in their own area was their own doing.

The number of dead appalled them. Burial of corpses in that warm weather was an urgent necessity. To the cemetery in the battalion's area the dead from all over Port Said were brought. They arrived in trucks, hearses, ambulances and even a Coca Cola lorry. Loads and loads of bodies, of all ages, and both sexes.

They were buried in roughly-bulldozed mass graves. The actual number of corpses created a great argument in Parliament, with the result that a Commission of Inquiry was sent out to verify the facts. It seems likely that the Commission's retrospective Report was optimistic, for the soldiers on the spot were in no doubt that a larger number of Egyptians had been killed than was estimated in the Report.

By comparison with what the Russians had done in Budapest a few days earlier this may not have been very many. Yet therein lay another facet of the tragedy of Port Said. The Russians had put down, brutally and mercilessly, an internal, purely Hungarian uprising. Tanks, firing phosphorus shells into street after street, had crushed the unhappy rebels and caused enormous casualties. All this had gone on with murmured protests only from world opinion and the United Nations. For world opinion had been confused by the Israeli invasion of Sinai, the bombing of Egypt and the launching of Operation *Musketeer*.

In a thick-skinned way the Russians are in fact sensitive to what everyone thinks about them. Had the world been slightly less distracted by our antics in Port Said the Russians just might have spared a few thousand of the lives which were snuffed out in Budapest that autumn.

Besides the dead there were many wounded in Port Said. Too many for the limited medical services to cope with. It was decided that the Surgical Team and section of 23 Parachute Field Ambulance, which had dropped with 3 PARA, should rejoin the remainder of the Field Ambulance which by now was in action in the town. Here, in the Fruit Market, they operated for several days, dealing with several hundred Egyptian casualties. Distribution of food to the local hospitals was another task which fell to the Field Ambulance. All offers of medical help were refused. It was perhaps reasonable of the Egyptians to be chary of allowing those who, by implication, had caused the wounds, to treat them. For to them the filthy British were responsible for it all. If there had been no invasion of Port Said there would have been no casualties.

An argument which contained a good deal of truth.

The Surgical team had moved in a 'borrowed' bus. This had bogged down in the soft sand when all the orderlies and stores were aboard. Mike Newall's Bren-gun carrier had been used to tow it clear, after which Malcolm Elliott had driven in a nightmare progress through the town, using sidelights only. They had dodged in darkness round shell holes, rubble and corpses.

By now 'borrowed' transport was in evidence everywhere. Ron Norman's batman was to be seen pedalling round on a stop-me-and-buy-one ice cream vendor's tricycle. Basil had come ashore with the gunners and was equipped with a magnificent new Packard. Some reports said that this had been acquired by driving it straight through the plate-glass window of the show-room in which it stood. Lawrence Scragg had liberated a Buick in a characteristic exchange.

He entered a garage with one of the battalion fitters, and spied the car. The proprietor said that no ignition keys were available. Whereupon the fitter fiddled with wires under the dashboard and started it up. He drove round to the petrol pump.

'No cars working. No petrol,' said the proprietor.

'Right. We'll put a grenade in the petrol tank.'

And suddenly he was filling the car up.

Transport throughout all units ashore was in some confusion. The vehicles had been loaded weeks ago, in Cyprus, Malta and England. Occasionally the loads were switched or cancelled. This state of affairs was pinpointed by an encounter between a high ranking staff officer and the driver of a three-ton truck. The truck was hopelessly jammed between the bows of a Landing Ship Tanks and a telephone pole on the quayside.

'Get this thing shifted! What's your unit anyway, and what are you doing here?'

'I can't move, sir. And my unit's back in the U.K. I'm the driver of the Officers' Mess truck.'

Which was true. By accident the truck had been sent on ahead. The cavalry regiment which owned it was still in barracks at Windsor.

As the days passed it was only comedy of this sort which blunted the revulsion and sense of frustration which everyone felt. No one could be quite sure what would happen next, but they all realised that what had occurred so far had been a futile and expensive waste of time.

Shooting accidents continued to dog the battalion. None of them was fatal. On the 4th day two men from Chris Hogg's platoon were sitting on the flat roof of a block of flats, cleaning their weapons. Suddenly a burst of Bren-gun fire from the block behind missed them by inches. There was an awkward moment next day when the Infantry unit relieving the battalion 'cleared' the buildings housing Support Company with machine-gun fire. Support Company, who had been in the battle from the start, were not pleased or impressed with this show of keenness on the part of the newcomers.

It was as well that the veil of secrecy and misinformation which had surrounded Operation *Musketeer* from the start, extended into the future. After a few days it became obvious that there would not be an atomic war on account of the battalion's efforts. But what was to follow was less clear.

The usual, inevitable rumours were rife. For one delirious afternoon it seemed likely that the battalion would return straight from Port Said to the U.K. aboard a troopship. The prospect of escaping from the damage, the flies, the smell, and the pathetic hordes of distressed civilians was welcome. It was not to be.

'A' Company had meanwhile been ordered to take up positions at El Tina, some fifteen miles down the Canal to the south. The climax of the cease fire negotiations had been a farcical front line, some six hundred yards wide. For the cause-way which links Port Said to the mainland of Egypt at this point is a strip of land containing the road and the banks of the Suez and Sweetwater Canals. Across the Suez Canal to the east is desert, leading to Sinai and Israel. To the west lies the boggy waste of Lake Manzala.

The Allied and Egyptian armies could only glower at each

other on this narrow peninsula, a mere ribbon on the map. The Egyptians did not confine themselves to glowering, but opened fire on numerous occasions. The British front line was held in the beginning by 2 PARA, who were dug in near the village of El Cap. As time passed a mass of barbed wire proliferated in no-man's land to their front. The Egyptian positions opposite were similarly protected. It seemed unlikely that either side could move, short of a major preliminary bombardment.

There was still talk of Russian volunteers and huge air reinforcements being flown to Syria from Russia, en route for Egypt. It may have been with these in mind, with a possibility of a major Egyptian counter attack at some time in the near future, that the orders to 'A' Company were given. They were instructed to prepare defensive positions at El Tina, a few miles behind the front line.

Mike Walsh and his second-in-command had a long day of it. They supervised the placing and digging of positions and then retired to the Canal Company house which contained the 'A' Company headquarters. There had been little sleep during the past few days. In the bedroom of the house was an enormous double bed, complete with brass knobs and a sprung mattress. With one accord they flopped onto it and were asleep in a matter of moments.

A jeep screeched to a halt outside a short time later and they awoke in some confusion. Into the room strode the Colonel who was deputy Commander of the Parachute Brigade and the Brigade Major, accompanied by a delightful and debonair French girl. She turned out to be a war correspondent who had thumbed a lift with them to the front. The chaos in which she found Mike's headquarters amused her a lot. Luckily the party was equipped with the comforts of warfare and, over one and a half bottles of whisky, El Cap, Port Said and the whole operation took on a rosier hue.

Journeys to El Cap provided incident on two occasions. Colonel Crook whirled back in great haste one evening after

187

visiting the company there. By now he was using a powerful and flashy Chevrolet which was not endowed with headlights. At 50 m.p.h. his driver was relying on the straightness of the road as they hurtled through the darkness. Suddenly there were shell holes all over the road, and they bounced and weaved their way precariously through them. Tony Watson, the signals officer, was less lucky. With his sergeant and driver he had been down to replace wireless batteries. Again they were returning in darkness, and too fast.

When they hit the rough patch of road the jeep careered off to the left. It sailed through the air for what seemed an age, describing a somersault as it did so. Upside down it crashed into the water. After a long time the four figures surfaced, still wearing their berets. The lights of the jeep still glowed in the depths.

They looked at each other and burst out laughing. But the humour faded from their faces when they realised that a walk of fifteen miles through the cold desert night lay ahead of them. They could not decide, in their dishevelled, soaking clothes, whether they had crashed into the Sweetwater or the Suez Canal. The difference was important. In the Sweetwater Canal the parasites which cause the serious tropical disease of Bilharzia are abundant. Tony and his party were anxious about every suspicious symptom they developed during the next months.

11th November was Remembrance Sunday, just six days after the landing at El Gamil. Horace McClelland went down to take the Service of Remembrance with 'A' Company. The smaller, intimate gathering of the company, the silent Canal where no ships passed, and the familiar prayers made a poignant scene. The Suez fiasco in a nutshell.

They all had much to remember.

Later in the day definite orders were issued for embarkation on the 12th. For 3 PARA at least the charade of Operation *Musketeer* was almost over. Rapidly the battalion packed and prepared to move once again. The captured *S.U.*100 was driven to the quayside and loaded aboard a landing ship. It was destined for the tank museum at Bovington where, I am told, you can still see faint 3 PARA markings inscribed on its sides.

The play was over, the actors were leaving by the stage door, but the audience was to go on clapping and booing for years. Mostly booing.

On board the *New Australia*, as she sailed back to Cyprus, the battalion was insulated from the consequences of its actions. What the world said lay, for the Toms, in the future. They could not foresee that what they had done would split conversations and produce heated arguments at home, would be reviled as an outdated piece of gunboat diplomacy, or, for the diehards, would be blamed only for its incompleteness.

'If only you'd gone on. . . .'

If only we had gone on, the best that could have occurred would have been a return to the tedious Canal Base from which Britain had thankfully retired two years earlier. The worst that could have happened would have been an atomic holocaust.

Eisenhower, the President of the U.S.A. at the time, said in his memoirs a few years later 'I've just never seen a great power make such a complete mess and botch of things.' He might have added that but for the United States' actions in July the whole affair would not have happened. But the soldiers returning on the troopship knew none of this. All they took back with them to Cyprus was the satisfaction of knowing that whatever had been messed or botched, their part of the show had been all right.

They had done what they were told to do. And of the 15,000-odd British troops who went ashore at Port Said they had been the first.

CHAPTER XI

AFTERMATH IN ARABIA

WHEN they returned to Famagusta they did not exactly find the red carpet put out for them for their pains. Rather the Red Caps. Military Policemen swarmed around and insisted on searching every item of baggage as it came ashore. They even frisked the men. This indignity proved too much for the Colonel, who ordered his battalion back to camp unsearched, on his own responsibility.

The reason for such an unwelcoming reception proved to have been the French. To *les Paras* it had all turned out to be another Indo-China, a second Algeria. Fight like hell. Win (or lose) the battle, and along came the politicians and give it all back to the enemy. Long experience had made them hard-boiled and realistic. As soon as they disembarked in Cyprus they had cashed their numerous souvenirs. Russian and Czech weapons had fetched enormous prices on the EOKA-run black market.

British troops, who at that moment disliked EOKA even more than they disliked their political leaders at home, were unlikely to do the same. The Red Caps were not to know this.

In hospital at Nicosia the wounded had already received visitors who, to them, were more welcome than the top brass and press correspondents who had arrived in the early days. As soon as the 'sea tail' of the battalion returned to camp they came to see us. They had been disappointed never to reach Port Said but more than made up for it by the care they now took of those who had. Richard Dawnay, the transport officer, and Ted Edwards, commanding the Rear Party, excelled themselves. Mail, messages and any requests were dealt with immediately by the efficient service they provided. 3 PARA knew how to look after its own.

Now we heard, from those who had just returned, all about the end of that confused week in Egypt. So the battalion returned to Tunisia Camp. And five days later I was allowed to rejoin them there. Looking around the dust and the teeming soldiers it was hard to believe that it had ever been. We might never have left this dreary, fly-blown place. Nevertheless I found out that everyone was preparing, in a disbelieving way, to take part in another airborne operation.

I was back.

Disillusion hung in the air, like the autumn rain-clouds which surrounded us. But there was nothing for it. We must make ready for whatever was coming next. I looked into the few wicker panniers of medical supplies which had returned from Port Said. These had travelled inviolate through the various searches under the protective cloak of the Red Cross.

Inside, shielded from prying eyes by shell dressings and bandages, I found a selection of Russian Carbines and sub-machine guns with enough ammunition to keep their owners in practice for years.

Yes. I was back with 3 PARA.

During the weeks that followed the extent of the ignominy gradually became apparent. I walked into the officer's mess tent for lunch one day.

'There's only one thing clear about this operation,' said a senior voice, holding the floor, 'and that's that this government isn't fit to run a kindergarten.'

And so it went on throughout the whole battalion. Incredulity, accompanied by a slow anger was the prevailing emotion. We did not yet know the worst. Did not know that a lukewarm homecoming awaited us in a country impatiently suffering from petrol rationing. Did not know that two years later we would be ridiculed in Jordan.

A corporal in the Arab Legion was speaking to one of the Toms on the edge of Amman airfield. It was the summer of 1958.

'But you can't be the battalion which jumped at Port Said! They were all wiped out by the Egyptians.'

Cairo Radio had rewritten that particular little bit of history very effectively.

However, in the last weeks of November 1956 we were spared all this. It was suggested that to pass the time, which was hanging heavy, the battalion should play a match against the French.

'What would they like to play?' The Colonel asked François, who was still with us.

'Well, sir, it is difficult. You see they have been fighting for six years and have not played any organised games during this time.'

Which made one think. It was not entirely surprising that, after competing unsuccessfully in the running Algerian débâcle for several more years, *les Paras* eventually revolted against their government. Granted enough provocation our own soldiers might well have done the same. We had been let off lightly.

Colonel de Fouquières, who had helped us so much with the timely landing of his Dakota, visited the camp a few days later. A very bibulous party it became. When viewed sufficiently darkly through a full glass even Operation *Musketeer* seemed a pretty good show. I endeavoured to interpret as the French Colonel waxed didactic. Finally, seeing I was in trouble, he said with a twinkle:

'*Alors, vous êtes le A.D.C. Vous êtes foutu.*' Which could be politely rendered, 'If you're the A.D.C. you've had it.'

In some disarray we saw him to his car.

Then there were inspections and speeches. The battalion was inspected or addressed by H.E. the Governor, by General Keightley, by the Brigadier, and by General Kendrew who had just assumed command in Cyprus. It was the Colonel's speech which made the greatest mark with the boys. He spoke briefly about the whole operation and explained how it had been curtailed. This, he said, was reason for gratitude on our part.

'We achieved what we were told to do,' he ended, 'and maybe it was all fairly good fun. But remember the price we had to pay. In two days' fighting we lost four dead and forty wounded. Ten days of that, and there wouldn't have been much battalion left.'

And, quietly, the crowd dispersed.

One evening the Officers' and Sergeants' Messes entertained the R.A.F. aircrews who had flown us. In the Dome Hotel in Kyrenia the beer flowed in torrents, and stories became taller as the evening wore on. I met the Squadron Leader who had flown Chalk Seven and thanked him for his encouraging words before we took off.

'It was very kind of you to say you'd cut the slipstream down for us, before jumping.'

'Oh we always say that. We can't do a damn thing about it really, but it's good for morale.'

The pace of the party quickened. A piano was produced, and songs began to unwind. Finally, after a lot of barracking, the Colonel was persuaded to sing *Frankie and Johnnie*.

At the last verse we all joined in.

> This story has no morals
> This story has no end
> This story only goes to show
> That there ain't no good in men.

The raucous chorus rang out over the harbour and re-echoed off the castle walls, cold in the moonlight.

No good in men. Too right there ain't.

*　　*　　*

Three years later I was demobbed. And I was a little more sober.

All in all they had been good years. The gloomy prophecy of 'dustbins and smelly feet' had not been fulfilled. Like a drone in a beehive I had made my brief flight with the army and sunk gratefully into obscurity.

By sheer chance I settled in General Practice in a garrison town where the Parachute Regiment maintains its Battle School. Such is the shortage of army doctors at the moment that we take sick parades for the soldiers each morning. From time to time familiar faces reappear and we talk of the good old days. Everyone appears to have risen a few ranks in the interval, the privates I knew are corporals, and the corporals are sergeants now. Otherwise it is all very much the same.

Some familiar faces can never appear on sick parade.

Ron Norman, who had survived so many battles, was killed when a helicopter crashed last year in Borneo. With him died Harry Thompson who took me through the rigours of 'P' company. All the time there is a constant erosion of the ranks by death and injury.

Pretend how you will, parachuting is not the safest of pastimes. Only twelve months ago a stick from 3 PARA, including the Commanding Officer, were dropped by night accidentally onto a railway line in Norfolk, in the path of an oncoming train. They escaped with their lives, but several were injured and scrambled out of their harnesses with seconds to spare. There was astonishment down the line when the express appeared, bedecked with parachute canopies.

This sort of thing is inevitable. There will always be accident and injury in training Airborne Forces. By their very nature the soldiers are accident-prone. They have been selected and trained for the forefront of battle and they accept the risks involved.

It is harder for their wives.

Not only do their families stand a higher risk of bereavement than most, they also endure more rapid, unpredictable and prolonged partings. Like all units of the Strategic Reserve, the Parachute Brigade is liable to be moved at short notice to any point on the globe. In the past few years 3 PARA have spent much time in Bahrein. Other units of the Brigade have been to Borneo, Aden, East Africa, Germany and final irony, back to Cyprus as the backbone of the United Nations peace-keeping force.

This story is theirs. Suez may be now, as Sergeant Sparvell of the Intelligence Section reckons, 'just a dirty word.' But in my brief time at Port Said I had seen much to be proud of.

General Hackett, now deputy C.I.G.S. is himself a survivor of Arnhem. In a recent lecture he crystallised the enigma.

'Though war may be bad, though application of physical force among men may be bad . . . the military life, which would disappear if violence vanished among men, is in many respects good. Why this should be so is not difficult to see if we look at what have been called the military virtues. . . . They include such qualities as courage, fortitude and loyalty.'

I had seen a good deal of all three both before, during and after Suez. I had watched while Teds were transformed almost mystically into Toms. The figures who stalked out of barracks in Aldershot wearing winkle-pickers and velvet collars were the same people who had lain bleeding and uncomplaining in the garage at El Gamil.

The senior Medical Officer at Arnhem had not found their forbears were plaintive either. And the legion who sleep beneath their crosses in the gentle turf of the Oosterbeek Cemetery need not be ashamed of their successors. Such is the compulsion of the brief and bloody tradition which they established in the second World War.

And it goes on. Sometimes in the last year or two I used to wonder if the new faces would prove as steadfast as the old ones had been. There is always the temptation to say that things are not what they used to be when you were there.

Early in 1964, among the new faces was a captain called Barry Jewkes. He had called in to sick parade to see about one of his men with an injured ankle. He was to go out shortly with 3 PARA for a year in Bahrein, and we talked about this and that:

people we knew in the battalion, rock climbing and the prospects in Bahrein.

'A pretty dead-end place, but we may be able to get away to Aden or Kenya.'

'Tell me about it when you get back.'

And he went out. Sick parade was succeeded by morning surgery. The routine of a day in the rain-washed market town rolled on. As spring came we had our own affairs to think of. The swimming bath appeal, the fête for the Freedom from Hunger Campaign, the production by the Little Theatre; all these absorbed us.

Barry Jewkes went away to different problems. But he won't be back to tell me about them. This is why.

3 PARA had flown to the treacly heat of Bahrein in early April and were quickly at home there. They built the camp a few years previously and knew it all only too well. It was welcome news to 'B' Company when a fortnight later they were briefed to move to Aden. A 'Company Group' with additional reinforcements was formed, just as a 'Battalion Group' had assembled for Port Said. There was a platoon from 'C' Company, a section of mortars and medium machine guns, a Parachute Regiment Air Contact Team and a detachment from the 23rd Parachute Field Ambulance. Company Sergeant Major Stead must have found these preparations familiar. It was he who, as a corporal with 'C' Company, had been rescued by Malcolm Elliott from the edge of shanty-town seven years ago. He had done it all before.

Major Peter Walter who now commanded 'B' Company group had been reared on this sort of thing for many years. Only a short time ago he had left the 22nd Special Air Service Regiment (22 SAS) whose very existence was quick moves by air. We had met briefly at dinner in Hereford, and I noticed the ribbons of the M.B.E. and M.C. on his 'blues' jacket. But I did not realise then how Churchillian his attitude to adventure was. A short time later, while on leave, he hitched a lift out to Brunei to join in the war there.

They all arrived in Aden by 17th April and were placed under the command of 45 Commando Royal Marines. Early the next morning training began in earnest, commencing with a session over the scramble course. The accent was on mountain warfare, field-firing and marching with heavy loads. They had been out of England barely a fortnight and were not fully acclimatised, but during that period of training not a single man fell out.

Once again it was Britain's obligations in the Middle East which were at stake. Once more, but indirectly this time, Nasser was the chief opponent.

Many years before the birth of Christ merchants and pilgrims used the road running north from Aden to the Yemen. This route was used to carry the perfume, spices, frankincense and myrrh of Zanzibar, Socotra and India to Petra and Damascus and then on to the Western World. Camel caravans moved out of Aden through the fertile basin of Lahej and wound their way through the foothills to the mountains of Thumair and Dhala and on into Qataba, well inside the Yemen border. Pilgrims travelled this road to Mecca. But it has never been a safe route. For centuries the tribesmen who live in the mountains flanking this road have menaced travellers, pilgrims and merchants and held them to ransom. The fiercest and most troublesome of the tribes are the Radfanis who live in the rugged 3,000 to 5,000 ft. high mountains east of Thumair.

The declared aim of the Yemeni Republic, backed by President Nasser and the United Arab Republic, is to destroy and take over the South Arabian Federation, the Aden Protectorate, and get rid of British influence in the area. The tribes of the Radfan formed a ready-made guerrilla force well able to assist them achieve their aim. Strategically they were well placed. Many of the tribesmen were therefore trained, armed, and financed by the Republican Army. A constant supply of weapons, ammunition and supplies were smuggled across the long and difficult border and thence along secret routes into the heart of the Radfan Mountains. In January 1964 the 'Red Wolves of the Radfan', as they boastfully called themselves, started their campaign to cut the Dhala road.

The Federal Regular Army or F.R.A. were quick to retaliate and in the same month struck back into Radfan territory but the effects of the campaign were short-lived. The main role of the F.R.A. is to protect the long frontier with the Yemen and no troops could be spared to garrison the area won. In February the F.R.A. were withdrawn and the situation steadily deteriorated. The Federal Government then requested the aid of British troops to quell the dissident activity and to safeguard the Aden–Dhala road which had been repeatedly mined.

So the British were preparing to undertake what was virtually an old-fashioned punitive expedition into this jagged maze of gaunt hills. As 'B' Company Group and 45 Commando knew well, the Middle East was apt to call for old-fashioned methods. Yet if much of it seemed familiar to them, there was an uncomfortable difference between the Radfanis and the Egyptians against whom they had both fought in 1956.

The Radfanis knew how to shoot.

During the first few days Major Walter and the C.O. of 45 Commando spent much time flying over the proposed area of operations. From the air the countryside looked like crinkled brown paper, stretching away endlessly into the haze of the Yemen to the north. But this is a vertical desert, and each crinkle is a tangle of burnt wadis and dry scarps of mountain running up to 5,000 feet.

The original plan was to drop the 'B' Company Group in darkness onto a D.Z. in the Wadi Taym in the centre of the area. They were to fly in two of the clumsy Beverley transport aircraft which had succeeded the Hastings. The D.Z. was to be marked by a small Pathfinder Force provided by 3 Troop of 22 SAS. But disaster overtook this party as they lay up in hiding the day before the drop was due. Surrounded and hopelessly outnumbered by dissident tribesmen they had to fight their way back out of the area, losing half their strength in the process. Their mission was impossible, and the drop was cancelled.

It was not a good start. The Company Group had been waiting all day to emplane, but then stood down late in the evening of April 30th. An hour later they were ordered to move north by road. The track was appalling, and the column of trucks was delayed by five separate punctures. Seven hours later, tired and dusty, they came to Thumair.

On May 2nd the action began. The company prepared to carry out a fighting patrol by night to the head of a pass some distance away in the hills. The artillery support was planned and the guns registered their targets for the night, firing a few rounds to establish the exact range of each one.

During this fire a group of men were seen dashing for cover into a deep wadi nearly two miles away. The Company Commander decided to capture the group, some of whom were obviously armed. A small patrol moved down behind them to cut off their retreat while Barry Jewkes and his men prepared to ambush them on the other side. Before the jaws of the trap could close the whole group dispersed into a nearby village. The Political Officer for the area for his own good reasons subsequently refused to allow the village to be searched.

Barry Jewkes' patrol cleared three other villages, all of them deserted, but the last recently so. In this main village near the head of the pass there were signs of a hurried departure and cooking fires still burning. Beyond the village the hillside was honeycombed with man-made caves, all prepared for defence, and all showing signs of hasty evacuation.

They had drawn a blank everywhere. But to emphasise that it was not over by any means, a number of ineffectual shots were fired at them on the way back to the company base.

Two days later came the main effort to subdue the Radfanis' territory. 45 Commando were to make a frontal sweep of the area, and 'B' Company Group were to infiltrate by night into the Wadi Taym—where they should have dropped a few days ago.

The long, twisting approach march in darkness was exhausting. But stray light signals flashing from the villages and mountains around their route kept them alert. Once they were in the Wadi Taym numerous figures carrying lanterns could be seen hurrying across their line of march. In the flickering lamplight it was possible to see that many of the figures were carrying slung or shouldered rifles. The dissidents were reporting for duty.

Opening fire on the enemy at this stage would achieve little. It was better to preserve secrecy. So the company moved in silence across the wadi, using footpaths, sometimes marching along bunds (narrow banks of stone or dried mud dividing the fields), sometimes across plough. Navigation was difficult, and one error cost them precious time. Their objective was the hills at the head of the Wadi. These overlooked the area originally planned as the D.Z. It was on those rocky hillsides that the S.A.S. party had fought desperately to escape a few days ago. The tribesmen who had attacked them had come from all the countryside around, and many had been based on the village which lay in the head of the Wadi. They were known to have decapitated the S.A.S. dead.

'B' Company had no illusions about their opponents, but still they did not fire. Often the Radfani lanterns bobbing past were only a short distance from the leading platoon. Time was critical, and any engagement now would waste it. They must be well on their way up the lower slopes before daylight. Even when two Radfanis suddenly rose like partridges nearby and ran away, nobody fired. Dawn was flickering, orange and red, hurrying them on.

By now the leading platoon were giving away no chances. They had deployed from single file and were moving forward singly in bounds, a method known as 'pepper-potting'. This exposes a target to the enemy for seconds only, as men run forward from one scrap of cover to the next. The Radfanis could see an apparently endless series of soldiers leaping towards them, as the red sun rose behind the mountains to the east. But daylight found the company on low ground, overlooked on every side.

Then the firing began. Shots came from several forts surrounding the village; from the hillsides above them and from groups of tribesmen behind in the wadi.

They were entirely surrounded by Radfanis. The leading platoon was in the worst position, close below the enemy on the hills, and overlooked by one of the ancient forts nearby. These forts have survived for hundreds of years, and their twenty feet thick walls have been found almost undamaged after attacks by rocket-firing aircraft. The platoon could only go to ground themselves behind the low bunds or attack the fort. They attacked.

They went forward in bounds, one section providing covering fire while another moved. All cover ended fifty yards from the fort. They threw several smoke grenades and dashed forward over the open ground. They fired their sub-machine guns through slits in the walls of the downstairs rooms and flung hand grenades into the courtyard. The platoon commander leapt over the wall and another grenade was flung down the dark passage which was the entrance to the fort.

The smoke and dust cleared after the explosion. Out ran one bedraggled chicken. The enemy had fled to the hills. The tension eased, but not for long.

For a number of Radfanis had moved out of the village to the south side of the wadi and were firing into the rear of the Company. This was particularly uncomfortable, since although the bunds gave good cover from the front they gave none from the rear. Two N.C.O's were wounded by this fire.

Meanwhile Barry Jewkes and his platoon, who were bringing up the rear of the column, came round the spur which had hidden the battle from them until now. Immediately they saw a party of enemy working their way round to fire on the company from behind. Barry Jewkes gave a quick order and the ensuing burst of fire accounted for four of the enemy killed out-right. The remainder went to ground behind a wall and returned the fire. Straightaway he led the assault on them and they broke cover and ran for it. Most of them were killed or wounded as they did so.

Radfani mortars opened up from a village behind them as they consolidated after this spirited action. Despite the vicious singing splinters, and flying rock fragments no one was hit. Methodically they laid out their fluorescent orange and crimson nylon air-recognition panels. While waiting for the ground attack aircraft to appear they engaged the enemy firing from the hillside above them.

It was not a long wait. The Hunters of 208 Squadron now repeated for the company all and more than the Fleet Air Arm had done for them at Port Said. With pitiless accuracy they dived again and again to blast the enemy forts with rockets and cannon fire. The tribesmen were driven from them into the hills. The most impressive air strike was made on a fort only 15 yards to the left and 150 yards beyond the Company tactical Headquarters.

It was about this time that a rocket or a mortar-bomb—no one was ever quite sure which—hit the Company H.Q. fort. Three men were slightly wounded. The Company H.Q. was without a set of air panels at the time. Private Pennington volunteered to return to the Company Sergeant Major and collect them. This was an exposed run of 300 yards. His friends watched tensely as the enemy bullets kicked up spurts of dust around him all the way down the slope and across the Wadi and back again. But he made it.

Gradually they cleared the village of enemy, killing several. In the hills overlooking the company a number of snipers remained well concealed. Hidden deep inside caves or in stone sangers they were hard to pinpoint. And their fire became increasingly accurate.

Barry Jewkes had come to Company Headquarters to report, with a small escort. Sergeant Baxter had also returned from his platoon at the opposite side of the village. Just as he left to rejoin his men the sergeant was hit in the chest. Two of the escorting soldiers were also hit, several times each. Barry Jewkes dashed out of the cover of the courtyard and dragged the sergeant to safety in the shelter of the wall. Helped by two soldiers he dragged in the wounded men also. As he stooped over the sergeant to give him an injection of morphia the upper part of his body showed above the wall for a few seconds.

A sniper's bullet hit him behind the ear, and he died instantly.

'We may be able to get away to Aden . . .'

From what I already know, there is much more to tell. How the two wounded were carried across 75 yards of open ground to the shade of the fort by Lance Corporal Bruton. Sergeant Baxter shot through the lung, was able to make his way somehow unassisted. Had they lain out in that scorching sunlight till evening none would have survived. Later in the morning an air drop of ammunition was arranged. One load fell wide and Private Davis was shot and killed as he went out with the retrieval party.

Towards sunset a Belvedere helicopter landed and evacuated the wounded, all of whom have now fully recovered. That was not the end of it. Later in the operation against the Radfanis, 'C' Company fought a similar battle, every bit as hairraising, but only one of their number was wounded.

Six decorations for gallantry have since been made to members of the Battalion involved in the Radfan fighting.

.   .   .   .   .

The commitment is endless. So far from fading from the face of the globe, the Queen's enemies seem to be increasing. But for most of us the early morning starts, the crashing aircraft, or the sniper's bullets are an unlikely hazard. We can now send our gunboats, our Internal Security Forces, or our punitive expeditions, from the firm base of an armchair at home. We shall send no one more often than the Airborne Forces. Inevitably they, not we, will pay the price. The 'mods' and 'rockers' who are Toms today will serve us every bit as well as the Teds a few years ago, who in their turn lived up to the standards of their forbears in the Second War. They are unlikely to let us down, for failure, except by annihilation, has not become a habit of theirs.

It is now rather for us, the civilians, the voters, the democracy, not to fail them.

APPENDIX

Positions in 1956 of those who appear in the story.

3 PARA

Battalion Headquarters

Commanding Officer	Lt.-Col. P. E. Crook, O.B.E.
Second-in-Command	Major D. S. Beckett, D.S.O.
Adjutant	Captain Gerald Mullins
Air Adjutant	Captain Geoffrey Howlett, M.C.
Signals Officer	Captain Tony Watson
Intelligence Officer	Lieutenant Jim Burke
Intelligence Section	Sergeant Sparvell
Regimental Aid Post	Sergeant Rabet
	Corporal Dunbavin
M.O.'s Batman	Private Holden

'A' Company

Commander	Major Mike Walsh
Platoon Commander	Peter Coates
Sergeant	Crompton
Private	Pugsley
Private	Clements

'B' Company

Commander	Major Dick Stevens
Second-in-Command	Captain Karl Beale, M.C.
Platoon Commanders	2nd Lieutenant Chris Hogg
	Sergeant Norman
Private	Lamph

'C' Company

Commander	Major Ron Norman, M.B.E., M.C.
Platoon Commanders	Lieutenant Phillip Butterworth
	Lieutenant Jack Richardson
Sergeant	Read
Corporal	Stead
Private	Penning

Support Company

Commander	Major Geoff Norton
Mortar Officer	Captain Norman Morley
Anti Tank Officer	Lieutenant Bill Hill
Machine Gun Officer	Lieutenant Mike Newall
Machine Gun Sergeant	Howse

Headquarter Company

Commander	Major Lawrence Scragg
Company Sergeant Major	Baker
Motor Transport Officer	Captain Richard Dawnay
Sergeant	Turkiewicz
Drivers	Smith
	Pearson
Quartermaster	Captain Bob Grainger
R.Q.M.S.	Chippy Robinson
Colour Sergeant	Bradley
P.R.I.	Major Noel Hodgson
Batman	Private Castelnuovo
Paymaster	Major Ted Edwards
Corporal	Brackpool

APPENDIX

OTHER UNITS

I PARA

M.O.   Lieutenant David Hartley
Padre   Horace McClelland
Platoon Commander Lieutenant Peter Chiswell

33rd Light Regiment, R.A.

M.O.   Captain Basil Shardlow

9 Squadron, R.E.

Troop Commander   Captain Jock Brazier
Second Lieutenant   Graham Owens

23rd Parachute Field Ambulance

Commanding Officer Lt.-Col. John Kilgour
Surgeon   Major Norman Kirby
Anaesthetist   Captain Malcolm Elliott
Section Commander Captain Maurice Fearnley
Private   Neill

Airborne Forces Depot

'P' Company Commander Major Harry Thompson
Sergeant   Crompton